THE
MAKING OF AMERICA
SERIES

SPRINGDALE
THE COURAGE OF SHILOH

HOME OF PETROSS CHISM. Located on Mill Street, it was called the prettiest home in Springdale in 1876. (Courtesy of Mrs. L.W. Searcy and Shiloh Museum of Ozark History.)

THE
MAKING OF AMERICA
SERIES

SPRINGDALE
THE COURAGE OF SHILOH

VELDA BROTHERTON

ARCADIA

Copyright © 2002 by Velda Brotherton.
ISBN 0-7385-2385-2

Published by Arcadia Publishing,
an imprint of Tempus Publishing, Inc.
2 Cumberland Street
Charleston, SC 29401

Printed in Great Britain.

Library of Congress Catalog Card Number: 2002106319

For all general information contact Arcadia Publishing at:
Telephone 843-853-2070
Fax 843-853-0044
E-Mail sales@arcadiapublishing.com

For customer service and orders:
Toll-Free 1-888-313-2665

Visit us on the Internet at http://www.arcadiapublishing.com

FRONT COVER: *SPRINGDALE FIRE TRUCK NUMBER 1. Around 1917, there was a dispute about the purchase of a fire truck for which firefighters had raised $265. The men threatened to resign unless the city bought a truck, and the council finally gave in and bought the combination hose and chemical Federal fire truck for $5,400.*

Contents

Acknowledgments		6
Introduction		8
1.	A Savage Place	10
2.	For Their Souls and Minds	22
3.	Trails, Rails, and Ribbons of Highway	41
4.	Build Us a City	52
5.	Serving the People	74
6.	Returns for Their Labor	91
7.	Law and Order, or Else	112
8.	That's Entertainment	121
9.	Guns of War	131
10.	Ah, Prosperity	145
Bibliography		157
Index		159

Acknowledgments

All history is viewed through the mists of time, and so facts sometimes become skewed, certainties become indecision. History can only be presented to the best of our abilities to reproduce another era long past. There will be those who feel that they could have presented certain passages with more acumen, wit, and truth. Any errors in this book are mine, and gratitude belongs to those who willingly helped me with such good humor and patience.

A huge bouquet of thanks goes to everyone who assisted in gathering the wealth of information necessary for this recording of Shiloh/Springdale history. Without the assistance of Bob Besom, director of Shiloh Museum, I would not have known where to start in collecting information. A special thanks to Librarian Manon Wilson and Assistant Librarian Sherry Raible for their support in locating photographs and bringing the images to life for these pages. Their untiring efforts will be forever appreciated.

The wealth of information contained in this book would not have been so readily available had it not been for the late Professor Walter Lemke, local historian and founder of the Washington County Historical Society, whose recording of Springdale history has been invaluable, and Bobbie Byars Lynch, whose endless research and records were a great help. The *Springdale News,* and its special editions tracing the history of the city since 1887, eased the search for materials and made for hundreds of delightful hours of researching the city's colorful past.

Books by local authors Bruce Vaughan, Herbert Gordon Holcomb, and historian Stephen Strausberg, who have recorded their families' lives in such detail, revealed little known tidbits of life in those early years. To each of them I am grateful.

To the countless others who put up with my incessant questions and telephone calls, I owe a special debt: Hollis Spencer of the Washington County Sheriff's Department; Jeff Harper, Springdale prosecutor; Cliff Palmer, pastor of First Baptist Church, retired; Chief Hinds, Springdale Fire Department; and Charlie Shields, Marketing, University of Arkansas Press. A special thanks to the ladies at the Art Center of the Ozarks for going an extra mile to provide me with a treasured photograph and trust I would return it to them. Nor have I forgotten all those who sent material that proved so useful: Sandy Prince at Northwest Arkansas Radiation Therapy Institute, Janet Edwards at the Rodeo of the Ozarks, and Dr. Charles Kelley, President of Northwest Technical Institute.

And last, not because that is his order of importance, but because he will understand being at the end of the list, a very special thanks to my patient husband, Don, who spent so many hours in the library and untold days, weeks, and months helping me research this information, so that I might present background material as correctly as is possible when it is blurred by the passage of time.

SHILOH MUSEUM CELEBRATES WITH STORYTELLING AND FOLK MUSIC FESTIVAL, 1996. The annual event benefits the museum's endowment fund. (Courtesy of Lucille McVay and Shiloh Museum of Ozark History.)

Introduction

In the wilderness of the Springfield Plateau, buffalo once grazed belly-deep in prairie grass, deer and elk roamed, rabbit and squirrel frolicked. To the south, the Boston Mountains of the Arkansas Ozarks rose like ancient sentinels against a crystal blue sky. The King, the Buffalo, the White, the War Eagle, all rivers nourished by springs and creeks that flowed from the oldest mountains in North America, their majestic grandeur long since eroded by time, found their mouths and journeyed to the sea.

Settlers arrived in the county briefly known as Lovely on the heels of the Choctaw, the Osage, and the Cherokee, then and forevermore removed to the Indian Nations a few miles to the west. These God-fearing folk had no notion that the first people to settle this land believed it could never truly belong to anyone.

Hungry for land to call their own, the settlers homesteaded the wilderness. Near an abundant spring of crystalline water, the newcomers carved out their farms, eagerly building homes on this plateau in the Ozarks of Arkansas Territory, with its lush land and abundant game, its pure water and virgin timber. Here, they would raise their families and grow crops in the rich soil. Through both hard and bountiful times, they would worship, toil, laugh, love, live, and die.

None could imagine the destiny of this humble settlement in the decades and century to come. They could not envision the bitter war that would rip their lives apart, setting brother against brother, and neighbor against neighbor. Nor could they guess that the apple seeds they planted with such care would one day bring fame and fortune to the town and ultimately create a foundation on which men of vision would build their empires.

Today, reminders of that first primitive church they called Shiloh stand as silent witness to the hardships endured and the sacrifices offered. The same rivers and springs fill sparkling lakes created by man. Sunlight nourishes the earth and sweet winds sing their songs, songs that remind us of who we were and what we have done.

And we must listen, for without knowledge of our past, we are nothing. We cannot stand alone against adversity or triumph without such support. If we do not believe in ghosts, then we must believe that the spirits of those who prepared this place dwell today in every blade of grass, every tree, river, and gust of wind. It is said that we do not die as long as someone remembers us and speaks our name. Here, we speak their names and remember, so that they and their deeds may live forever.

HOLCOMB SPRING LOCATED ON MILL STREET. *The spring was used as a water supply into the 1950s before the demand became too great. (Courtesy of Bobbie Lynch and Shiloh Museum of Ozark History.)*

1. A Savage Place

But what is civilization? Is it a practical knowledge of agriculture? Then I am willing to compare farms and gardens of this Cherokee nation with those of the mass of the white population in the Territory... Does it consist of morality and religion? Our people have built, wholly at their own expense, the only meeting house in the Territory.
—Cherokee Nu-Tah-R-Tuh (No Killer)

The place of which Nu-Tah-R-Tuh spoke was his home, land of the northwest Arkansas Territory. His people, known as the Western Cherokee, were about to lose that home, as had the Osage and Choctaw before them. Yet another treaty would be broken to open this rugged, remote country to the white man, whose need to settle land west of the Mississippi appeared insatiable.

A savage, unforgiving land, the rugged Ozarks were once relatively level countryside, which erosion carved over eons into rough mountain-like terrain to form the oldest range on the North American continent. In northwest Arkansas, elevation drops from 2,250 feet above sea level on Mount Gayler in the Boston Mountains to the rolling country of the Springfield Plateau, which is only rarely interrupted by higher elevations than its 1,350 feet.

The first people appeared here as the glaciers from the Pleistocene Epoch retreated, eons before the hardy pioneers arrived. The Paleo Native Americans found a barren, Siberian-type landscape. They probably hunted musk oxen, mastodons, and other Pleistocene animals. They must have been nomadic hunters, who followed the big game animals, for the presence of such large animals leaves little wild plant life. Sparsity of artifacts suggests that population densities were low. And soon, they either died out or moved on.

About 10,500 years ago, the large, fluted lanceolate-shaped points, remnants of these earliest residents, were replaced by what are called Dalton points. The striking change marks a significant cultural shift among the prehistoric peoples in northwest Arkansas, a transitional stage between big game hunting and the hunting and gathering orientation. This long Archaic Period was followed by the Woodland Period when the region was largely a prairie habitat moderated by a trend toward more rainfall. The resulting oak and hickory forests are still typical of the countryside today.

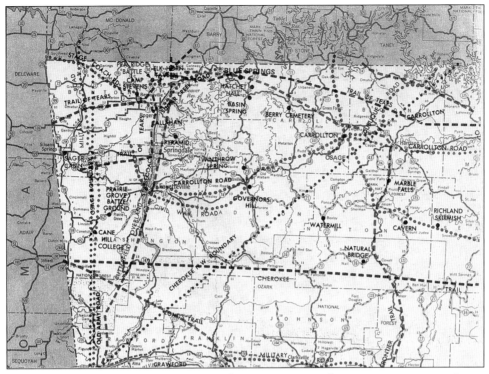

OLD TRAILS, TRACES, AND ROADS, OVERLAIN ON A LATER MAP OF THE AREA. *This map shows routes of Native American travel through northwest Arkansas before white settlement.*

Roughly 800 years before the arrival of the white pioneers, the Mississippians were part of a far-flung network of complex Native American societies. These societies were prosperous and well organized, and the people were farmers, not too different from the white men who would come along much later. They cultivated maize and other plants. Hunters and gatherers continued to thrive, but the fertile river bottom lands were filled with a variety of domesticated plants that would prompt the establishment of permanent villages.

What happened to these people and why didn't modern Native Americans meet up with them? In 1541, Spanish conquistador Hernando de Soto, who had landed on this country's shores in 1538, reached the Mississippi River and beheld the land of these early people, a land that would one day become Arkansas. He explored the White River to its source and might have caught brief glimpses of these people as they moved furtively through the wilderness.

In 1673, Jesuit priest Jacques Marquette journeyed to the Arkansas River to spread Christianity to the Native Americans. He found clusters of wattled cabins and encountered Ogupas, or the downstream people. The name was changed to Kappas or Quapaws, and their land was called Arkansea, or Arcana, the land of the downstream people. From this came Arkansaw or Arkansas.

These explorers couldn't know that the diseases they carried were unknown to these native peoples, and that their mere passing meant extinction for an entire race. With no immunities to the strange germs, most suffered unimaginable deaths. Within 100 years of early white contact, 95 percent of the original population was destroyed by disease.

The Osage Native Americans trod the wilderness of the Ozark plateau of northwest Arkansas as early as the 1600s. The Osage could not be considered settlers, for they only passed through, hunting the area that teemed with game, fresh water, and virgin timber. But others did put down roots in the land. Shawnee, Delaware, and Choctaw villages were established near an abundant spring where Shiloh would one day prosper. As early as 1806, a large band of Cherokee left their eastern lands to settle along the many waterways on this piece of land, a part of the Louisiana Purchase of 1803. They had traded to the government some 6,000 square miles in two large tracts from that part of the Cherokee Nation in Tennessee and Georgia, in exchange for lands in northwest Arkansas.

In 1813, warfare between the Osage and Cherokee prompted the government to assign William L. Lovely as an agent to the western Cherokees. In 1816, Lovely obtained an unauthorized purchase from the Osage that became known as the Lovely Purchase. It included what is now Benton, Carrol, Madison, and Washington Counties and was known for a short time as Lovely County. However, the actual western border of the Cherokee reserve was not surveyed

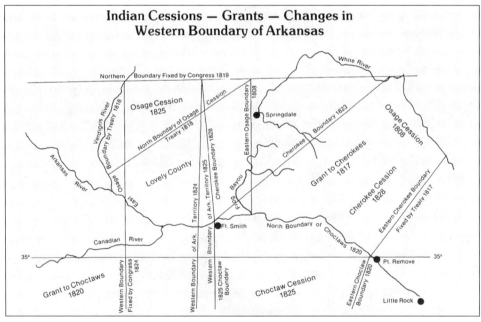

INDIAN CESSIONS, GRANTS, AND CHANGES IN THE WESTERN BOUNDARY OF ARKANSAS. *The boundary was changed several times before the final boundary between Arkansas and Indian Territory was established.*

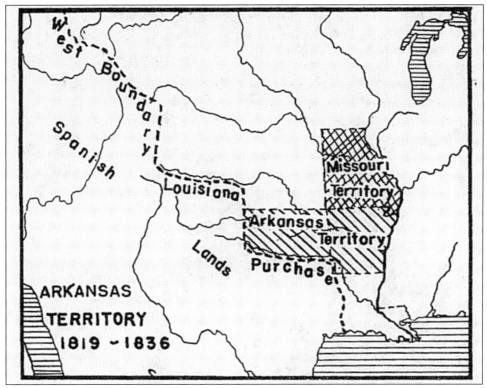

ARKANSAS AND MISSOURI TERRITORY WITHIN THE BOUNDARIES OF THE LOUISIANA PURCHASE, 1803. *The government surveyed the Territory of Arkansas in 1831 and established township and section lines that still exist today.*

until 1825 and left deliberately vague, for west of it lay the untamed Indian Territory, now Oklahoma.

The Cherokees were promised that they would have no limits to the west and that they would not be surrounded by white people. In December of 1817, a military post was established in Fort Smith. For the time being, whites were not allowed to settle the lands and the United States Army was ordered to evict white squatters. Historians have pointed out that many Cherokees were married to whites, making it difficult to say whether the first settlers in the county were really white or Native American, or a mixture of Native American, African American, and white.

Historian Bobbie Byars Lynch says, "To say that these educated Cherokees stayed confined in an invisible line is closing our minds to history." She believes there were settlers of mixed ancestry, including whites, in the area as early as 1808. For many years, these first settlers lived much as the early natives had.

Extremely fertile soils and a natural flow of springs proved to be an invaluable resource for those early settlers. Valuable year-round flows from larger springs could power mills to grind the corn they would grow in the rich earth. Beneath the ground lay deposits of coal and precious metals. In his journal, written while he traveled through the Ozarks in 1818, Henry Schoolcraft described the living conditions of these earliest settlers:

> He had several acres of ground in a state of cultivation, and a substantial new-built log house, consisting of one room which had been lately exchanged for one less calculated to accomodate [*sic*] a growing family . . . the boys were clothed in a particular kind of garment made of deerskin which served the double purpose of shirt and jacket. The girls had buckskin frocks, which it was evident . . . were intended to combine the utility of both linen and calico, and all were abundantly greasy and dirty.

Schoolcraft went on to describe the state of the interior of a cabin. On the walls were hung the horns of deer and buffalo, rifles, shot-pouches, leather coats, dried meat, and other articles. Also displayed was great evidence of a skill in the fabrication of household furniture. He also described a dressed deerskin, seamed up to nearly resemble the animal from which it had come and filled with bear's oil, and another filled with wild honey.

A year later, a white explorer by the name of Frank Pierce fought his way up the White River, trapping and hunting to stay alive. When he reached the mouth of the West Fork of the White River, he ascended the stream to within 2 miles of where Fayetteville is located today. He saw no roads or clearings, or even a log cabin where he might seek shelter. He did discover a herd of buffalo, but curious Native Americans sent him seeking the cover of a nearby bluff. Entranced by the land, he would return nine years later, by which time much had happened to make living in the area safer, not to mention legal, for the white immigrant.

As a clamor arose to remove the Cherokee, this letter appeared in the *Arkansas Gazette* from Cherokee Nu-Tah-R-Tuh (No Killer):

> But what is civilization? Is it a practical knowledge of agriculture? Then I am willing to compare farms and gardens of this Cherokee nation with those of the mass of the white population in the Territory . . . Does it consist of morality and religion? Our people have built, wholly at their own expense, the only meeting house in the Territory.

In due time, a line was established between the Indian Nation to the west and Arkansas Territory—that border had been changed so many times it was difficult to keep track of—and the latest treaty agreement with the Native Americans was abolished. The whites were given permission to live in the region and settlers trickled in. Still, Lovely County remained a borderland, sparsely populated and perched on the political boundary where the United States ended and the Indian Nation began.

Many of the early settlers of the Springfield Plateau made their homes on land once included in the Choctaw Land Grants, referred to as the Dancing Rabbit

Creek treaty of 1830. In that year, over 300 Native Americans of an unknown tribe camped on Spring Creek, which flows along today's Mill Street in Springdale. Many had acquired 40-acre homesteads through the treaty and sold them to white settlers.

The government surveyed the Territory of Arkansas in 1831 and established township and section lines that still exist today. When the area around Shiloh was surveyed in 1834, surveyor's notes indicated 6 farms and 100 acres under cultivation, but only one name was recorded: James Fitzgerald, son of John. Three log cabins could be seen along the section line that runs today along Maple Street. Cultivated land was noted in the line that runs close to what is today's intersection of the Old Missouri and Old Wire Roads.

A German explorer, Friedrich Gerstaker, who roamed through Arkansas in 1838, wrote in his journal about the living conditions he found:

> In a lean-to of rough-hewn logs, protected on only three sides from wind and rain, the woman lives not days or weeks, but months or sometimes even years under conditions that would destroy the health of a European.

Those who settled Shiloh fared better, but not much, as they built their log cabins from the surrounding timber.

Land patent dates are misleading, in that they do not indicate the time of first settlement. It was often to the settler's advantage not to file until he had to in

PAINTING BY LOCAL ARTIST E.A. DOEGE. *This wonderful work depicts Shiloh and the surrounding farms prior to the Civil War.*

order to avoid levied taxes. Some might live on their homesteads as long as 40 years before filing. Sometimes, claim jumpers would file on their homesteads, then sell them back to the owner at a profit.

Goodspeed's History of Arkansas declares that settlement of Springdale (Shiloh) began around 1838 and it was "due to religious purposes" with the immediate reason being "the noble spring near a tree across the road." However, John Fitzgerald once told a Fayetteville news reporter that he came to the area in 1825, actually before it was legal for white men to settle here. Some historians disregard reports from those who claim they lived in the area prior to the removal of the Cherokee, but many family records indicate those early settlements did exist.

Sometime before 1839, Fitzgerald and his wife, Mary, established an inn near what is now the intersection of Old Wire Road (Telegraph Road) and Old Missouri Road (Springfield Road). Cherokee, making the deadly march from their homes to the south and east along the Trail of Tears that same year, stopped to rest at Fitzgerald's Inn. Later, the inn would become a regular stop for the famed Butterfield Stage Line. Fitzgerald and his wife operated the inn until 1861. Their children, Isaac, James, Joshua, and John, filed on nearby land in 1838 and 1840.

In 1858, the Butterfield Stage Line came within a mile of the settlement and designated Fitzgerald's to the east as a stage stop. The Lovelady Inn in Shiloh was a mile or so off the route, but was often used as a place where passengers could eat and rest. From all accounts, this was the first tavern in town and, after the Civil War, a portion of it would become the Gladden Hotel, often referred to mistakenly as the first tavern in town. The coming of the stage promoted business growth and provided mail delivery to Lynch's Prairie Station, a small structure along the stage line and the first post office to serve the community.

LYNCH'S PRAIRIE POST OFFICE, 1859–1866. *The post office was established with the arrival of the Butterfield Overland Mail route and closed soon after the Civil War. (Courtesy of Mrs. L.W. Searcy and Shiloh Museum of Ozark History.)*

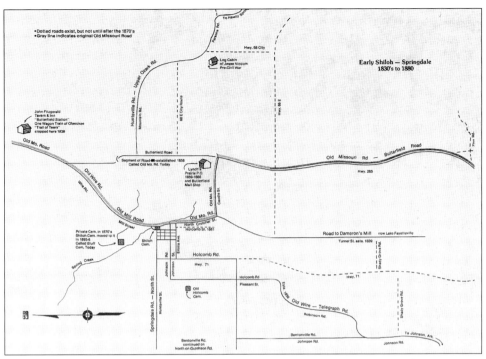

MAP OF EARLY SHILOH/SPRINGDALE FROM *1830* THROUGH *1880*. *The grey route marked is the Butterfield Stage Road. Dotted lines show the original route of Highway 71 and 68 when they were built.*

William Davidson Quinton, his wife, Sarah, and their family joined the Fitzgeralds in 1840, migrating from an earlier settlement on the West Fork of the White River to the south. Attracted by the abundant water and lush farm land, they set up house along the banks of Spring Creek. Quinton, who had strong ties with the Primitive Baptist Church, donated a piece of land on which he hoped a church would be built. The land grant issued him, signed by President John Tyler, is dated March 10, 1843, and covers an 80-acre tract.

It was there, on the banks of this stream, that the idea of Shiloh would take root and grow, but not until the arrival of a charismatic man by the name of John Holcombe. Other very early settlers were the Graham family, S. White, and Spencer Forby Fine and his wife, Jane. Soon, Holcombe, an active member of the small Primitive Baptist Church in the settlement of West Fork, purchased or traded for 600 acres of land from Quinton and Fine, and moved his wife and 14 children to their new home on Spring Creek.

Holcombe is considered to be the founder of Shiloh. In 1840, after moving from West Fork to his new home, he organized a church, which he called Shiloh. It formed the religious cornerstone around which the town would grow. Though he and his family continued to attend services in West Fork for a period of time, Holcombe also became an important part of Shiloh. Soon, a log church was

17

JOSEPH HOLCOMB, 1896, MAYOR OF SPRINGDALE. *Often referred to as the father of Springdale, it was Joseph's father, John, who originally platted the town. (Courtesy of Mary Frances Page and Shiloh Museum of Ozark History.)*

erected and, in 1843, he began to take part in services on a regular basis. According to church records of the West Fork Primitive Baptist Church, at the beginning of each worship service, an elder or member would be requested to speak to the congregation. Holcombe was always eager to answer that call.

For a time, everyone in the vicinity of the community on Spring Creek referred to the tiny new settlement as Holcombe Springs, but the name Shiloh soon caught on, and the area would be called Shiloh until 1872. For nearly 20 years, this original group had the place pretty much to themselves. Cattle were pastured on the town site and wild animals drank at night from the stream that ran through what is now the business district. The untamed wilderness country in which those first settlers made their homes was cut by numerous buffalo paths, with the main herd located a few miles northwest of the future town site. There were a few bears, but the timber wolves were thick. During the hour every evening when the wolves began to howl, each family would blow a horn to start the dogs to barking and keep the wolves away. If one of the families did not blow their horn, someone went to investigate the reason.

Inevitably, others would find this paradise, but discovery was slow in coming. A man named R.S. Coon arrived and built the first mercantile, locating it in close

THE SECOND SHILOH PRIMITIVE BAPTIST CHURCH. *This church was built in 1868 after the original log church on the same site was burned during the Civil War. It served as the first public school until 1885. (Courtesy of Washington County Historical Society and Shiloh Museum of Ozark History.)*

THE BAGGETT FAMILY. *From left to right are (front row) two unidentified young men, Myrtie E. Baggett Fitzgerald, Arminta Belle Baggett Lichlyter, James Blake Baggett, and Margaret Lichlyter Baggett; (back row) A. Dyal Baggett and Louis Blake Baggett. Others are not identified. (Courtesy of Lichlyter collection and Shiloh Museum of Ozark History.)*

proximity to the Primitive Baptist Church. An 1855 issue of the *Southwest Independent*, a weekly Fayetteville newspaper, ran an ad for Stone and Holcombe indicating a wide variety of staples, dry goods, books, and hardware for sale at their store in Shiloh. Before further settlement could evolve, however, the dark clouds of war gathered on the horizon.

Events leading up to the Civil War put all considerations of building a town aside. Caught between the North and the South, residents suffered dreadful losses. What the Federals did not burn, the South destroyed to prevent the enemy from profiting from the "spoils of war." The Shiloh Baptist Church was burned, along with several other homes in Shiloh. Many families fled the area, including John Holcombe and his family. Most of the town was burned to the ground. Until that bitter conflict ended, there would be no future for the tiny settlement on the banks of Spring Creek.

In 1866, John Holcombe and his family returned to Shiloh from Texas to rejoin the sons who had fought in the Civil War. He built a home on the hill near the site of today's Legion Hut and immediately began plans to rebuild the Shiloh Primitive Baptist Church. Upon the charred remains of Shiloh, residents set about resurrecting their town.

One of the first buildings to rise from the ashes was Shiloh Church, completed in 1868. It would serve not only as a church, but as a school. It was soon sold to the school and, a scant three years later, with the town growing around it, another church house was built on land donated by Holcombe. It was shared by Methodists, Missionary Baptists (today's First Baptists), and other congregations, as well as the Masons. The building remains standing today near the corner of Huntsville and Main Streets in Springdale's Shiloh Historic District.

In 1868, Holcombe drew up the first plat of the town. Six lots made up the original plat. Some deeds were not recorded, but the first transactions contain two names: Spencer Forby Fine and William Davidson Quinton. On that city plat were the following names and transfers of property: Spencer Forby Fine; William Davidson Quinton; William D. Quinton and wife Sarah; John Holcombe and wife Dorthea to James Baggett; John Holcombe to S.S. Purcell; John Holcombe to William Holcomb; James Baggett and wife Margaret to Asa Boydston; Jo Holcomb and wife Belle to Asa Boydston; Asa Boydston and wife Elizabeth to P.M. Ownbey; A.W. Boxley and wife; and F.L. Brooks to Thomas Gladden.

In 1870, Joseph Holcomb—by now he had dropped the "e" from the spelling of the family name—returned to Washington County and purchased from his father the old homestead. Jo had lost his beloved wife, Cener, but in the span of time at Mineral Springs, he married again. His purchase included rights to the plat of the town, laid out by his father in 1868. In 1872, he was elected clerk of Washington County and served four years.

The founder of Shiloh, John Holcombe, died on December 9, 1876, one day short of his 79th birthday and two years before the incorporation of the town he had helped create.

Baggett and Lichlyter, Blacksmiths and Wagonmakers. From left to right are the following: M.B. Lichlyter, ? Tollman, Jonathon Smith, and unidentified. (Courtesy of D.D. Deaver, Lichlyter collection, and Shiloh Museum of Ozark History.)

2. For Their Souls and Minds

Elder Mahurin was appointed moderator for the day and visiting brethren were invited to a seat in the council, a door was opened for the reception of members, called for the peace of the church and the conference was closed in peace.

—February 1845, Shiloh Church records

Once, John Holcombe stood on the banks of Spring Creek and envisioned a church where many would one day worship. In the song of the crystal clear waters, he heard voices raised in praise and glory. In the tall grasses and forests of oak and hickory timber, he spoke with his God and imagined the faithful walking where once great herds of buffalo grazed. On that day so long ago, a dream was born, a dream of a community where men, women, and children would come together, united in Christ, and where they would enjoy the fruits of their honest labors.

Upon this simple foundation, Holcombe nourished a city filled with churches of many denominations, the first of which was called Shiloh, a name taken from his beloved Bible. Within his dreams of this great church where all could worship, he placed his hopes for peace and prosperity. His son Joseph would see that his father's dream became a reality. The town was founded upon its church and when the country's Civil War destroyed that simple log building, they built another. The city would rise around it.

Holcombe's dream of a church became the Regular Baptist Church at Shiloh and, later, the Shiloh Church of Regular Baptists. John Henry Bookout, son of the last clerk, kept the records that date the church's beginning and the constitution being drawn up on August 22, 1840. The building later came to be known as the Primitive Baptist Church and had as its elders Samuel Wheat, William Poston, and John Holcombe. Deacons signing the constitution were John Wood and Berry D. Graham. No original membership roll was included.

In the first of the three church record books, along with a list of 336 members, are reasons listed for various dismissals from the origin of the body until 1879. Most stated, "Deceased, 1875" or "Departed this life, May 1847," but some read "Excluded, 1869," as if a member might have sinned in some way never to be revealed. Many of the names found in the membership list are familiar today, such

EMMA AVENUE, EARLY 1900S. *When churches were first formed, they grew up around the square, but soon the city would move and desert that square. (Courtesy of Vaughan, Applegate collection, and Shiloh Museum of Ozark History.)*

as Graham, Easley, Tisdale, Holcombe, Ingram, Sharp, Fitzgerald, Thornsbury, Bishop, Atwood, and White. Slaves of members are listed among these.

The first entry recorded a meeting of the church and is dated on Saturday before the Second Lord's day in February 1845. The ink on the now yellowed and brittle page is barely legible, but it appears to report that Elder Mahurin was appointed moderator for the day and visiting brethren were invited to a seat in the council. A door was opened for the reception of members, calling for the peace of the church, and the conference was closed in peace. Monthly meetings were held on the Saturday preceding the second Sunday of each month. Exceptions were made for bad weather and, later, the Civil War, during which time the church was burned.

Through Holcombe's efforts, the Shiloh Church was rebuilt in 1868. A story is related of how John Holcombe was riding a steamboat on the Red River in Texas and noticed the bell being used on the boat. He asked the captain if he could purchase the bell for a church he was planning to build in northwest Arkansas. Though the captain rejected the offer, when Holcombe reached his destination, he found the bell packed among his possessions. Obviously, the generous captain did not want to make a scene about accepting money for the bell and so chose this method to donate it to the little church.

After the war, the church flourished, but by the late 1800s, members were passing to their reward faster than new members were joining. No effort was made to attract younger members and a strict doctrine led the church away from evangelism, which some claimed caused the decline in membership.

FIRST BAPTIST CHURCH. *This church traces its roots to the original Shiloh Primitive Baptist Church. It was originally organized as the Landmark Liberty Church in 1870. (Courtesy of Bob Besom and Shiloh Museum of Ozark History.)*

In 1894, the graves in the old Shiloh Cemetery near the Primitive Baptist Church were moved to Bluff Cemetery, including that of John Holcombe, who passed away in 1876. In 1905, citizens organized an association to see to the care of Bluff Cemetery. Mrs. Charles F. Renner was elected president; Mrs. B.F. Deaver was secretary; Miss Georgia Harris was treasurer; and C.G. Dodson, J.P. Stafford, and W.H. Searcy were appointed to draw up a constitution and bylaws.

By 1927, there were only 40 members remaining in the church and records began to read "No Church in April," then "No church in June," and finally, the congregation met for the last time on the second Sunday of September 1936. Only four years from having reached its 100th anniversary as a church, the Shiloh Church of Regular Baptists ceased its meetings, its building was sold for improvement taxes, and the few remaining members moved on to worship with other churches in the area. Nevertheless, the legacy of John Holcombe would live on in the many churches erected within the growing city. Several actually had their beginnings in the humble Primitive Baptist building called Shiloh. The name remains and that building stands today as a reminder of those humble beginnings, so that history may never let us forget.

The First Baptist Church was organized as the Landmark Liberty Church by a gathering of 13 people on Saturday, February 19, 1870. Elder G. Bryant presided with B. Putman serving as clerk. The 13 charter members present were William Hunter, John Lichlyter, Louise Lichlyter, Margaret Fitzgerald, Elizabeth Fitzgerald, Margaret Baggett, Lurindia Baker, Fanny A. Putman, A. Lynch, Jacob Lynch, Isaac Lynch, Phebe Lynch, and William M. Blakely. Later that year, Putman was appointed the first pastor. The congregation met in a log house in Shiloh owned by the Primitive Baptist Church.

Church minutes of July 1871 state that the church agreed to build the fourth part of a "Church House" to be owned by the Regular (Primitive) Baptists, the Landmark (Missionary) Baptists, and the Methodists, while also being used by the Masonic Lodge. William C. Lichlyter and William A. Hunter were ordained as the church's first deacons. The Liberty Baptist Church would pay one-fourth of the cost and use the building one Sunday per month; the Methodists would put up one-fourth and use the church one Sunday as well; and the Primitive Baptists would pay half the cost and use it two Sundays. Since the Primitive Baptists met only one Saturday and one Sunday a month, they rented their other Sunday out to the Presbyterians.

In 1886, the Liberty Baptist Church changed its name to Springdale Baptist Church. John Mayes was its pastor then. A new building was completed in 1899. In the 1940s, the church once again changed its name to First Baptist Church with a sharp increase in membership. A mission church on Berry Street was established in 1932, another mission on Caudle Avenue in 1946, and another on Elmdale in 1960.

In 1954, work was begun on the first of a three-part master building plan. In 1955, the sanctuary, with a seating capacity of 1,000 people, was completed and the second part of the building program was started, the remodeling of the old auditorium into a chapel. The third part, the educational unit, would eventually house Shiloh Christian, the largest private school of its kind in the area. In the fall of 1979, a two-building worship center was completed and in the fall of 2002, a new building will be added.

The First Methodist Church was organized and utilized its partial interest in the Shiloh Church Building, holding services there until 1884 when a building was erected on Emma Avenue. Its first pastor, the Reverend Arthur Marston, transferred from Texas in 1890 when Springdale was made a station. In 1936, the land was sold to the federal government for a post office and a new building was erected on Johnson Avenue and Main Street. In 1930, the Methodist Episcopal Church united with the Springdale Methodist Church.

The Presbyterian Church was founded on May 1, 1882. After meeting in the Primitive Baptist Church building for a year, the congregation moved into a brick building erected for the church's use. When the Presbyterian Church disbanded in 1930, a small group of women, who composed the Missionary Society, along with other women of the town, carried on the work of the women's organization for 20 years. For carrying on fine work without having a church organization or pastor, this group of women was recognized both by the presbyterial and synodical. In 1950, the group became the nucleus of the reorganized church.

After determining that there was sufficient interest in reestablishing the church, the presbytery authorized the organization of the First Presbyterian Church in Springdale. On June 4, 1950, church school classes and worship services were begun in the civic club rooms of the public library until the new church could be built. Reverend Charles Douglas Brewer was active in the planning and building project. Twelve men donated labor, another cut the cost of earth moving, and another paid the entire cost of paving the church's streets on both Quandt and Young, as well as the parking lot. Women made choir robes and equipped the kitchen. Most of the windows, the pulpit, the organ, the offering plates, and some equipment are memorials. Its beautiful stained-glass windows were designed and built by a retired artist living in Arkansas and the large window at the front of the church was donated by the Madison Avenue Presbyterian Church in New York City.

Churches, other than those that shared that first Shiloh meeting place, soon formed as the town grew. Lutheran immigrants from North Carolina and Tennessee

FIRST UNITED METHODIST CHURCH. *This denomination also met in the original church building constructed by John Holcombe. In 1884, parishioners raised money to build a church on Emma Avenue. (Courtesy of Springdale Chamber of Commerce and Shiloh Museum of Ozark History.)*

First Presbyterian Church, 1962. Disbanded in 1930, the church was reorganized in 1950 after its members were held together by a group of active women who carried on their work for 20 years. (Courtesy of Donna Charlesworth and Shiloh Museum of Ozark History.)

moved into the Whitener community and Hindsville, and they organized the Whitener Salem Lutheran Church. For unknown reasons, probably because they did so much business in Springdale, they moved their meetings there. The Salem Lutheran Church is located today on the extreme western end of Emma Avenue.

D.A. Wellman and J.W. Scoles and their wives arrived in town from Battle Creek College, Michigan, in June 1884. They began erecting a tent 40 feet in diameter on the Holcomb property near the railroad track. Townspeople at first expected a circus. When they learned it was a religious service conducted by Seventh Day Adventists, the tent filled the first night. Crowds increased nightly and the meetings continued into August. By then, 74 persons had signed the covenant promising to keep all 10 commandments and asking for an organized church. Most of these were baptized at Stultz Mill Pond (known later as Shiloh Springs) northwest of town. Services were held in a rented building after that until, in 1886, a building was erected near where the tent had stood on land donated by Jo Holcomb. Members established a church school of ten grades in 1896. Eventually, it closed but was reopened in 1942 as an elementary school, offering eight grades of academic work. In 1945, the church building was moved to a quieter part of town where it could hold Saturday services in relative peace.

Mr. and Mrs. F.C. Ritter began Bible study groups in their home in 1908. In 1914, the *Photo Drama of Creation* was shown there. Unusual for that day, it contained not only picture slides, but also moving pictures synchronized with phonograph records in the form of recorded talks and music. It was not until 1933 that the Bible students adopted the name "Jehovah's Witnesses."

After a series of meetings held in the city auditorium, the Church of Christ was organized in 1912. When members purchased the meeting house of the North Methodist congregation on Holcomb Street in 1929, it became known as the Holcomb Street Church of Christ.

As the years passed, fewer new churches were formed. It seemed most residents were content with the ones they had. Occasionally, a revival would be held and a church would grow from that, like the Assembly of God Church, which was organized following a three-month revival in 1932. The church grew successfully over the years and, in 1958, a 450-person-capacity sanctuary was completed on West Huntsville Avenue.

Best known for the principle of triple baptism and its unusual method of observance of the Last Supper, the Dunkard Church of the Brethren opened its doors for a short time in 1910. The Dunkard Church originated in Germany in 1708. Though a building was erected on Berry Street, most of its members died or moved away, and the structure was sold in the 1930s to Berry Street Baptist Church.

Berry Street Baptist Church, organized in April 1932, originally met in an old store building, but moved on several occasions. Congregants once met for a time in the Seventh Day Adventist Church building, with the Adventists using the building on Saturday and the Baptists using it on Sundays. Members later moved into the old Dunkard Church Building. In 1952, 20 years after the mission was established, it was organized as a church. In 1960, the old educational part of the church was destroyed by fire. The new sanctuary was saved and what was burned was soon rebuilt.

During World War II, only two churches were established: Immanuel Baptist Church, in 1942, at the Legion Hut with 15 charter members present, and the non-denominational Jesus Name Church. In June of 1945, with the war coming to an end, the Gospel of Peace Church was founded.

With the Italian settlement of Tontitown so near, it was inevitable that a Catholic Church would soon open its doors in Springdale. Saint Raphael's Church was established in 1949. Reverend L.H. Schaeffer, pastor of Saint Joseph's at Tontitown, presided at the organizational meetings. The first Mass was held on December 4, 1949, in the Chapel of the Callison-Sisco Funeral Home. In February 1950, the church announced that the mission would be known as St. Raphael's Cenacle, which would meet in a redecorated house loaned by Mrs. Josephine Braun. On July 5, 1953, Ann Elizabeth McGetrick, daughter of Mr. and Mrs. J.P. McGetrick, was the first child to be baptized at Saint Raphael's. The mission was dedicated in March 1955 by Archbishop William D. O'Brien. In November 1958, the new structure of brick and stone, erected on a 30-acre tract on Highway 68 West, was dedicated.

During a revival in 1949, there were 21 conversions, which formed the nucleus for a new church organized as an Independent Fundamental Baptist Church, the first of its kind in northwest Arkansas. Known as the Temple Baptist Church, it

First United Methodist Church. In 1930, the Methodist Episcopal Church united with the Springdale Methodist Church and a new church was built on Johnson and Main in 1936.

moved from Sonora to Maple Avenue in Springdale in 1950. At a meeting of the First Methodist Church, members decided that another Methodist church was needed. A layman called the pastor and offered to supply funds for the erection of a church if a lot was purchased. Wesley Methodist Church was organized. The building was erected and the first worship service was held there on October 22, 1950. Early in 1954, ground-breaking ceremonies were held for the construction of an educational building to adjoin the original church structure.

Christian Science church members began to have regular meetings in private homes in 1951. As interest increased, a regular Sunday school was opened for children and the group moved to the Civic Club Rooms of the public library. Seven years later, the church was recognized as a branch of The Mother Church. In 1955, the church leased a historical building on Johnson Avenue. The 100-year-old building originally housed John B. Steele's general store and post office and it had no plumbing. The members went to work on the project of restoring it, however, and first services in the renovated building were held on February 6, 1956.

Saint Thomas Episcopal Church was formed when three devout ladies, Mrs. Louis Heerwagen, Mrs. Earl Heagler, and Mrs. Roy J. Bowman, organized an auxiliary on June 10, 1952. The group met regularly and finally increased its membership to 12 people. The local group became affiliated with the Church of the Redeemer in Rogers in 1953 and became known as Saint Monica's Chapter of the Episcopal Church of the Redeemer. The chapter continued its work in

FRIENDSHIP BAPTIST CHURCH AND CEMETERY IN SONORA, 1962. *This church continues to serve parishoners in the Sonora area. (Courtesy of Bruce Vaughan and Shiloh Museum of Ozark History.)*

Springdale until, eventually, a few other Episcopal families moved in, and, in October of 1956, the first service of morning prayer was held in the Civic Club Rooms of the public library. In December of that year, a petition was drawn up to form a church, and, in 1958, 5 acres of land were purchased for the purpose of erecting a parish house that could be used temporarily for services and church school until such time as a church and church school could be built.

The 1950s would continue to see the formation of churches. Free Holiness Church was organized in March of 1952. In line with their beliefs, the local group supplied a storehouse with food and clothing for assisting each other in case of emergency and other needs. First Landmark Missionary Baptist was organized in December 1954; the Pentecostal Church of God of America first met in the fall of 1954; and East Meadow Missionary Baptist Church, a mission of the Immanuel Missionary Baptist Church, formed in the fall of 1955. Congregants of the People's Mission, organized in 1958, met in an old upholstery building until the new building was erected a year later.

The Church of Christ (on North West End Street) was organized in September 1959. Some members of the new Church of Christ were formerly members of Holcomb Street Church of Christ.

Because of continued growth, the First Baptist Church opened Elmdale Baptist Church Mission in October 1960. By 1961, the mission had become a full-fledged church, and three more churches had opened their doors in town: East Side Assembly of God, United Pentecostal Church, and a Primitive Baptist Church.

In the early days, with travel so rigorous, even impossible for some, there were many tiny communities where a church and school served local residents. Churches grew in settlements that are, for the most part, gone now. Some have been absorbed into the city limits of Springdale, others simply outlived their usefulness and faded into oblivion, while still others continue to serve a congregation.

For a short time, Elm Springs to the west of town was actually a larger settlement than Shiloh. The Elm Springs Methodist Church there claims to be the oldest in the area, with services dating back to 1830. The first new member recorded was Margaret S. Webster, who joined in 1834. It is believed that the first pastor, Reverend H.G. Joplin, held those early services in the home of one of the ministers until about 1850 when a small building was erected. The church was burned during the Civil War and it would be several years before it was rebuilt near the site of the present building. Church minutes date back to 1882.

In 1883, something was to happen that might have shaken the faith of less devout members. On the last night of a revival in 1883, two intoxicated men from a neighboring community decided to disturb the large crowd gathered at the meeting. When no one paid attention to their disturbance, they left and returned with loaded firearms. One woman jumped out a window. Amidst the screaming and havoc, some of the men attempted to subdue the intruders, while others pulled firearms of their own, creating an Old West–style shoot out. Several injuries resulted, but the most seriously injured was one of the two who started the trouble in the first place.

The Goshen Methodist Church, southeast of Springdale, is believed to have been organized in 1832. James M. Burks deeded 11 acres of land for the church. The original log structure was blown away in 1882 or 1883, and services continued in the schoolhouse until 1884, when the church and the Masonic Lodge built a two-story building.

Friendship Baptist Church was organized in 1847 and is considered the oldest church in the Washington-Madison Baptist Association (Southern Baptist Convention churches). It was first organized as the Friendship United Baptist Church of Christ and, at the time, was located 3 miles southeast of Springdale.

In the days when 50¢ likely represented a day's labor, many church members paid by subscription in order to see a new church built. Nevertheless, the churches did get built. In March of 1888, Elder G.P. Hanks and some followers organized New Hope Baptist at Stony Point. By April, land was acquired for a building that was possibly erected the following year. (Records are sketchy.) One member paid his pledge off 50¢ at a time. On April 6, 1889, the building committee paid out $33.50 to cover the cost of shingles, windows, and doors for the church.

Pilgrim's Rest Free Will Baptist was organized in September 1911. In the first half of the twentieth century, the church had a total of 402 members. Records show that a Mrs. Shetley named the church, but the church clerk, Mrs. Harry

Wright, pointed out that Pilgrim's Rest was already the name of the school district. No one remembers for sure how the unusual name originated.

Some meeting houses began under one banner, but shifted to another. Silent Grove Community Church began as a Baptist Church in 1909, but, before it was completed, members realized that they were too few in number to carry on a church program. The denomination was discontinued and everyone interested in the community, regardless of denomination, decided to band together and begin a non-denominational church. The building was completed and a board of trustees was appointed in 1912. Today, almost all denominations are represented in church attendance. Preachers of several denominations, including Baptist, Methodist, Dunkard, Mormon, and others, have at some time preached in this church.

In the Ozarks, there was a community every 8 miles, more or less. It would include, in the least, one building for church, school, and community functions, and a general store. For the most part, these earliest churches were either some form of Baptist or Methodist sect, or were nondenominational. Circuit riding preachers visited communities throughout the county, carrying the Methodist doctrine. Many held services in brush arbors, under trees, or on the banks of a river where baptisms took place. It wasn't unusual for crowds of 50 or more people to gather for these baptisms, which called for total submersion in the waters. Often, they were all-day, gala affairs.

In the earliest days of settlement, schools were an integral part of churches, and vice versa. Where a school building stood, church services were most often also held. Education of the mind, heart, and soul were the goals of these hardy pioneers. They could not and did not separate them. The structure was shared out for the good of all; hence, the formation of the one-room school. Schools can trace their origin directly to the founding of the first church in most towns in Arkansas.

Even as they built their homes, toiled in their fields, and established businesses, education remained of utmost importance in the minds of settlers. As early as 1829, counties were assigned an obligation toward the schools. The Territorial Legislature passed the first law concerning public education, which required all county judges to appoint a trustee for the 16th section of land in each township, this section having been set aside by the federal government for public schools.

In 1843, the General Assembly passed a law that authorized a commissioner in each township that had 5 households or 15 children. Each of the qualifying townships was a school district authorized to elect three trustees, who were empowered to erect a schoolhouse, select a teacher, and begin school. Classes could begin as soon as funds became available from the sale or lease of the land, taxes collected in the township, and from subscriptions. The schools were to be operated a minimum of four months each year. In 1853, the legislature passed a school act that provided for the election by the people of a county school official and designated his title as county common school commissioner. Probably the earliest elected commissioner in the county was Peter P. Van Hoose.

Schools in the county were, for the most part, subscription schools. Only those who could afford the tuition could attend. It was not until 1867, during

Reconstruction following the Civil War, that the legislature enacted a public school law that provided for the election of the superintendent of public instruction and enacted a two-mill tax, with the proceeds to be used for public schools. In 1868, general funds were tapped for public schools and a poll tax was established. Every adult male resident was assessed a $1 poll tax and a property tax was authorized to pay for the support of a three-month-a-year school. By 1870, the state had begun to apportion state funds to the counties, and a large number of schools then came into being. Until districts were formed and records kept, little information on earlier subscription schools is available. For that, we must depend on the recollections passed down through families.

From the beginning, schools were plagued with problems. Some did well to remain open for three months and pay a teacher. As quickly as some school districts were formed, they dissolved. Annexation and consolidation continued to be the quick fix of financially troubled schools into the twentieth century.

Marlon Mason, the Johnson correspondent for the *Springdale News*, wrote in 1889 about his school days:

> Oft at night I lie awake thinking of the days that have been. Mr. Black with his long white hair, which gave him a patriarchal appearance, won the love and esteem of his pupils by treating them kindly; Roberts, who let the scholars do as they pleased; Inman, who had a fine for every little misdemeanor, who gave hard lessons and expected them to be got-all, all

BAPTISM AT A CAMP MEETING AND REVIVAL, C. 1900. *Baptisms and revivals were well attended by one and all, with no thought to denominations. (Courtesy of Bank of Eureka Springs calendar and Shiloh Museum of Ozark History.)*

pass in review. When future years roll around and better days come, the present house may be replaced by a larger, more substantial one, but the future is as a sealed book, and no one knows today what is to be tomorrow.

A perfect example of the one-room school is Old Stony Point. Built in 1881 and 1882, the room measured 20 feet by 28 feet. Later, a 14-foot addition, plus 4 more windows, making 9 in all, were added. There were 20 seats and 7 blackboards. The school at Harmon was built in 1867 of logs cut from the grounds and hauled from the Van Winkle Mill near Eureka Springs. Students sat on split logs to study from such texts as McGuffey's readers, the Blue-back speller, and Ray's arithmetic. One teacher taught anywhere from 15 to 60 students in grades one through eight. Often some students were older than their teacher, who may have received his or her certificate at the age of 16.

Mass consolidations in 1949 closed almost all the one-room rural school houses. A few remained scattered about the county, but by the late 1950s, teaching in one-room schools would be a thing of the past. The only remnants of those lost days are the structures that survived and are still in use as community buildings.

While most communities combined school and church in one building, it is strange to note that Shiloh may have been the exception. The first school was probably held in the Jo Holcomb home when he brought in a teacher, J.C. Floyd, to teach a small group of children. Floyd was later elected as a congressman.

SPRINGDALE HIGH SCHOOL. *Once known as Central School, today the school serves as the administration building for the public school system. (Courtesy of Mrs. L.W. Searcy and Shiloh Museum of Ozark History.)*

PARADE ON EMMA AVENUE, EARLY 1900S. No matter how far apart the early communities were, everyone was eager to come together for the most popular event, a parade. (Courtesy of Bruce Vaughan, Applegate collection, and Shiloh Museum of Ozark History.)

However, in 1872, when Shiloh rebuilt its church in the same style as the one built during Reconstruction, the old building became the public school until 1885. There is no record to show that school and church were ever both held in the same building.

In 1873 (some date this at 1871), the Baptist Church founded an organized school, purchasing land on the corner of what is now West Johnson Avenue and Highway 71B. A two-story brick building was erected called the (Shiloh) Missionary Baptist College, where today's school administration building is located, on the corner of Johnson and Highway 71B. "College," however, was a misnomer, for teachers taught classes from grammar school through the first year of high school. An enrollment of 40 pupils paid $2.50 per month each to attend. In 1885, the building was sold to the Lutherans. The upstairs was used for church purposes. In two rooms downstairs, the Reverends Rader and Bartholomew taught subjects, such as algebra, philosophy, literature, and religion. In 1895, the building sold again for $2,500 to the Springdale College Company, of which Millard Berry was president and C.C. Phillips was secretary. Seaton E. Thompson taught and conducted a private high school for two years.

In 1898, Josiah H. Shinn, educator, author, and former state superintendent of public instruction, came to town. He acquired the building and campus and set out to raise money with which to equip a school. He had visions of making the town a great educational center.

There were four teachers in his "first class school": H.F. Smith taught science and ancient languages; Miss Helen King taught modern languages and music;

SHADY GROVE SCHOOL, DISTRICT 36, EARLY 1900S. *One-room schools such as this served the many residents in outlying areas as both a school and church until mass consolidations in 1949. (Courtesy of Lloyd O. Warren and Shiloh Museum of Ozark History.)*

Mrs. Lee Sanders taught vocal culture, reading, and elocution; and Shinn taught the remaining subjects, including a teacher training course. Later, household economics, good morals, and gentle manners were added to the curriculum. There were 25 pupils, boys and girls, studying from seventh grade through two years of high school. A preparatory school for college was also offered. The school proved very successful for the short time it was open. In one year, enrollment increased from 25 to 80 students. Even so, by 1901, Shinn ran into financial difficulties and gave up, whether from poor management or some families' inability to pay, no one really knows.

When Shinn departed, Millard Berry acquired the property under foreclosure. Through his interest and leadership, and with the assistance of other school board members, including W.B. Brogdon and Dr. Christian, the first free public high school opened in the fall of 1901. The graduating class of 1903 had five members.

A grammar or elementary school was held in an old frame building that had been erected *c*. 1868 for a grammar school. It was replaced in 1885 by a two-story, four-room brick structure that stood on Allen Avenue facing Holcomb Street. Some years later, it was doubled in size. Until 1929, the building was used as a grammar school; then it was dismantled in 1940.

Until 1910, the high school used the old brick structure of the various colleges that had owned it. It was torn down and a new brick structure was erected on the site. In 1910, the school term was increased from seven months to nine, and a full four-year course was offered in place of the two-year course. After 1929, it was used as an elementary school, known as Central School. The building is used today as the administration building for the public school system.

New school districts were laid out in 1923. By 1937, 1,000 students were enrolled in the Springdale school system. In 1938, the elementary housing problem was addressed when Jefferson Elementary School, housed in the former administration building of the Migrant Labor Center, became a part of the Springdale school system. In 1947, the first of a series of building projects was begun. An eight-room elementary school was built north of Central and was named North Central. It was the first school to contain a lunchroom. For a time, the overcrowding problem was eased.

A big change came over the Springdale school system in 1946 when Elm Springs, Stony Point, and Peaceful Valley districts petitioned to be taken into the district, designated as District #50. In 1947, a state law was passed requiring all schools to be in a district containing a high school. This law brought about a rash of petitions for consolidation that, by 1949, had seen 22 schools brought into the system in the two-year period. This list contained the following names: Steele,

ZION SCHOOL, INCLUDING DIRECTOR WILSON CARDWELL. *This picture was taken some time after 1900. State Senator Cardwell was a descendent of early Arkansas pioneers and was born in Zion in 1868. (Courtesy of Shiloh Museum of Ozark History.)*

Spring Creek, Silent Grove, Tontitown (Smith's Chapel or Wood's Chapel), Brush Creek, Harmon, Zion, Accident, Hickory Creek, Sawyer, Fishback, Sonora, Habberton, Oak Grove, Shady Grove, Bethel, Monitor, White Oak, and Mountain Home.

A September 1961 news article might have been remiss in declaring Springdale's new high school as a $1 million structure, but it wasn't far off. The building project, some 77,260 square feet, cost a bit less than $900,000. A portion of the old three-story junior/senior high school, built in 1929, was utilized for the new school. A cafeteria, library, office area, and more classrooms were added. Over the years some of the older buildings have been demolished. As enrollment grew, several additions of classrooms were necessary, as well as the construction of bleachers, a gym and stadium, auditorium, and science and music facilities. In 1991 the buildings were air conditioned. Today 2,400 students attend classes in the 410,000-square-foot school, and there's little room left on the site for expansion.

Shiloh Christian School, a private school founded and sponsored by the First Baptist Church, opened in the fall of 1976. The school offered families an alternative to the public school system. Oakley Long came out of retirement from public school teaching to help get the school started. Pastor Cliff Palmer, now retired, believes that many families need their children to get an education from the standpoint of developing a Christian world view, rather than the world view offered by public schooling.

Originally teaching kindergarten through sixth grade in the old building of the First Baptist Church on Holcomb, the Shiloh Christian School moved into its

FIRST BAPTIST CHURCH. *The original members met in the first log structure of the Shiloh Primitive Baptist Church. They also founded Shiloh Christian School.*

GROUNDBREAKING CEREMONIES FOR NORTHWEST VOCATIONAL TECHNICAL SCHOOL, 1974. *Now known as Northwest Technical Institute, the school serves more than 6,500 students. (Courtesy of Shiloh Museum of Ozark History.)*

new building, adjacent to the First Baptist Church, in the fall of 1979. Today, it has an enrollment of between 800 and 900 students in classes ranging from four-year-olds through the twelfth grade. It is the largest private school in the region. "When we first opened the school," said Reverend Palmer, "it was an unusual concept, and enrollment was a bit slow. Seven to eight years later the Christian school concept was a great movement."

The Northwest Technical Institute (NTI) was created by legislative action in 1973 to serve the people of northwest Arkansas. The legislation's purpose was to create a school that was committed to working with business, industry, and the community to develop training programs that would create a skilled, productive workforce. Construction was begun in April 1974, and the school opened its doors in August 1975. At the time, it was virtually alone in Springdale's industrial park on Highway 265. Originally known as Northwest Vocational Technical School, the first building of 25,000 square feet serviced 115 students in seven course programs. Today, the campus has grown to 89,176 square feet and has over 6,600 students enrolled in 15 vocational diploma programs, 4 associate of applied science degree programs, and 4 technical industrial classes. All are transferable to the education degree programs at the University of Arkansas. Free adult education classes and classes through the Business & Industry and Extension program are also offered. James Taylor served as director until 1988. The current director is Dr. Charles Kelley. NTI celebrated its 25th anniversary in the year 2000.

Sports have not always been accepted in high school and, at one time, football was relegated to playground recess status. Even as late as 1911, the school principal was against the game. Probably the greatest football team to come out of Springdale High in those days was the 1944 team coached by Earl Voss. He and his boys won 11 games without a defeat and captured the conference title. Today, the Bulldogs enjoy great popularity and football is the number one sport at Springdale High School.

Basketball is also a favorite sport. The earliest record shows the Bulldog boys basketball team dropped their season opener in 1930 to Elm Springs, 24-9. Girls basketball was played as early as 1905. In 1910, the girls won 13 games in a row and captured the state championship. In the 1943–1944 school year, the boys Bulldog team was Northwest Arkansas Conference and District 1A champions with a 20-7 record. Betty Sue Heerwagen was all tourney for the fourth straight year in the Northwest Arkansas Invitational.

With the steep rise in population after World War II, the need for schools increased enormously. Many other changes faced the schools of that era, as the boom times forever altered the face of a city moving into years of growth and prosperity.

SPRINGDALE HIGH SCHOOL, 1968. *Today, 2,400 students attend the expanded 410,000-square-foot school. (Courtesy of Springdale Chamber of Commerce and Shiloh Museum of Ozark History.)*

3. Trails, Rails, and Ribbons of Highway

From stage-coach to truck lines, from muddy lanes to hard-surfaced highways, from isolation to neighborliness with the nation, Springdale has come in less than 60 years. What changes the next 60 may bring must challenge the imagination.

—Springdale News, 1937

Old Wire Road, cut from St. Louis to Fort Smith in 1830, was one of the first roads to accommodate Springdale traffic. The road was so named because it was used as the line for the telegraph wire from Jefferson City, Missouri to Fort Smith. From Shiloh, it was 12 miles to Fayetteville on the Old Wire Road. The road continued to be used as a local stagecoach road until some time after the city was incorporated in 1878.

The Butterfield Stage Line became the first east and west mail and passenger service on March 3, 1857. A cross-country mail contract had been offered to the line that could make the run in 25 days each way. Service had to begin within 12 months of the contract being awarded. The first line, dubbed "The Jackass Line," failed to meet the requirements, and a bid was then awarded to John Butterfield.

Butterfield had some 2,800 miles of route surveyed, purchased land for stations, and mapped out river and mountain crossings. The firm purchased 1,200 horses and 600 mules, branded each with an OM (Overland Mail), and shod and distributed them to the 141 stations. Over 1,000 men had to be hired and trained to serve as superintendents, conductors, drivers, station masters, veterinarians, blacksmiths, and wranglers.

Orders and specifications were drawn for over 250 regular coaches, special mail wagons, freight wagons, and water tank wagons. Coaches were painted either red or green and the running gear was bright yellow. The colorful coach, inscribed with the OMC (Overland Mail Coach) insignia on the doors, weighed 3,000 pounds and had a load capacity of 4,000 pounds. It carried six to nine passengers inside and an unlimited number on top. Celerity wagons or mud wagons were also purchased for use on the rougher sections of the route, which included the difficult Boston Mountain Crossing south of Shiloh.

Springdale Depot. This picture is taken from a postcard mailed to Evalyn Howard from Carl L., dated August 4, 1912, at 7 a.m. (Courtesy of W.G. Howard estate and Shiloh Museum of Ozark History.)

The stage did not run directly through Shiloh, but stopped at relay points and post offices and, besides carrying passengers, allowed settlers to communicate with the outside world in a way they never had before. After making its stops through Missouri, the stage crossed the border to John Fitzgerald's station northeast of Shiloh. Mail was delivered to Lynch Prairie Post Office several miles away, the nearest thing to a post office Shiloh would have until 1872. As mentioned previously, one of the favorite stops of passengers was the Lovelady Inn (later the Gladden Hotel) in Shiloh because of its excellent food, and, though it wasn't on the stage route as an official stop, drivers often detoured to allow passengers to rest and eat. Butterfield Stage Line operated until 1861, when the Civil War put the company out of business.

Railroads attempted to criss-cross the country as early as 1849. The Civil War temporarily put a stop to the movement. Laying of the rails actually began as early as 1849, when the war with Mexico ended and the gold rush to California began. People all over the country demanded rails from coast to coast. The St. Louis San Francisco Railway Company (Frisco) was born from that need, but only following long struggles over a period of many years. When the Frisco did finally spring to life, the small settlement of Shiloh would grow at a rate no one could have expected. Not even John Holcombe, whose dream had birthed a city, could have imagined such an expansion when he first set foot on the fertile soil and tasted the sweet spring water.

When interviewed for the 1937 anniversary issue of the *Springdale News*, J.F. Harris, one of the oldest living citizens at the time, claimed to have heard every

Baptist preacher of the old Primitive Baptist Church. Yet, he did not get to see the Frisco engines pull in for the first time in 1882 because he was working on the railroad south of West Fork. In that interview, Harris vividly recalled the early days of the town when the stagecoach was its only means of commercial transportation. He described the city as he saw it upon his arrival in 1874, saying, "There were no streets laid off, no railroad; and the major part of our present town site was either in wooded thicket or open fields." He recalled harvesting hay where Emma Avenue runs today.

The Frisco railroad line traces its history to March of 1849, when the Missouri Legislature granted a charter to the Pacific Railroad Company of Missouri. Leaders in the new enterprise were Colonel John O'Fallon, prominent St. Louisan, and Thomas Allen, influential state legislator. O'Fallon, the first president of the Pacific Railroad, was shortly succeeded by Allen. The Pacific Company was chartered to build a railroad from St. Louis to the western boundary of the state, there to meet any line that would be built east from the Pacific Coast. The projected route was from St. Louis to Jefferson City, to Sedalia, to Independence, and to Kansas City. By 1850, surveys were underway for the line and construction began on July 4, 1851. At that time, there was no railroad west of the Mississippi and none extending to it from the east. On July 23, 1852, the first 37 miles of the railroad opened to Pacific, Missouri, then known as Franklin.

Even before that opening, the Pacific Company had obtained legislative authority to construct a branch line to leave its main projected route at Franklin and extend to Springfield and southwest Missouri. The new line was called the

FRISCO DEPOT, TORN DOWN IN 1982. *It has since been replaced by Arkansas & Missouri Railroad. (Courtesy of Irene Carter and Shiloh Museum of Ozark History.)*

FRISCO DEPOT. Wagons filled with crates of peaches wait on the dock for shipment. This picture is from a postcard dated 1914. (Courtesy of Martha Brogdon, Earl Jones, and Shiloh Museum of Ozark History.)

southwest branch of the Pacific Railroad and it was the branch destined to become the nucleus of the Frisco system. Work was begun in June 1855.

By December of 1860, the Frisco line opened to Rolla, which would become the main terminus during the Civil War, though the railroad had been completed to Kansas City by 1865. Confederate troops inflicted such damage on the railroad that the southwest branch defaulted on their indebtedness to the state of Missouri and were separately sold to satisfy the lien. General John C. Fremont purchased the branch and reorganized it as the Southwest Pacific Railroad. Having acquired great wealth from the discovery of gold in California, Fremont obtained a federal land grant of millions of acres with which he proposed to continue the southwest branch all the way from St. Louis to San Francisco along the route of a survey he had completed as early as 1845.

By 1868, Fremont had failed financially and the South Pacific Railroad Company was formed to take over the line from the state. The line was extended from Rolla to Lebanon in 1869, to Springfield in 1870, to Pierce City in 1870, and grading was completed to Seneca, Missouri, on the Indian Territory border. The line lay just to the north of Shiloh.

After many changes in ownership and financial difficulties, the Saint Louis & San Francisco Railroad Company came into existence in 1876. By that time, Shiloh had changed its name to Springdale and, two years after the Frisco was officially a railroad, the city would incorporate. In 1880, construction was begun in Arkansas and reached Springdale in 1881, forever altering the future of that growing settlement. Without the railroad, it might have remained a sleepy small town, with few opportunities for growth, but the arrival of the Frisco Railroad allowed the farmers to ship hundreds of carloads of apples, strawberries, peaches, tomatoes, and, later, grapes and poultry.

The railroads also fueled the boom in the timber business. In the period between the late 1880s and the 1920s, railroads were using 3,000 hardwood ties for every mile of track laid. Sawmills were hard put to meet the demands of such construction. Ties were cut until there were few suitable trees remaining. Over that short period of time, millions of dollars worth of hardwoods were cut and shipped on the St. Paul Branch of the Frisco to Fayetteville. The 100-foot-high virgin forests of white oak, with their ash-colored, ragged bark, had been growing here long before the white settlers arrived. The stately monoliths had survived the days when the pioneers and their slaves cleared land for farms, a time when birds like the ruffled grouse and wild turkeys roamed free through the forests.

The arrival of the railroads changed the situation and the trees fell victim to the increased demand for ties. One by one, the magnificent giants crashed to the ground under the attack of the axe and saw, until only saplings remained. When the timber was gone, so was the timber boom. And so, too, were the branch railroads. One by one they shut down, steel rails were ripped out, and soon weeds hid the ties so there is little sign that they ever existed.

The wealthiest person in northwest Arkansas in 1882, at the time of his death, is said to have been Peter Van Winkle, the owner of a sawmill at War Eagle. Well aware of the value of the railroad to his business, he had been one of the biggest proponents for bringing the Frisco to northwest Arkansas. His large, steam-powered sawmill was located on the White River, just downstream from what is now the Horseshoe Bend recreation area on Beaver Lake. Nevertheless, the Frisco would continue to flourish along its run through Arkansas. At one time, there were six passenger trains a day traveling south to Fort Smith and returning.

There were bound to be train wrecks, and many are recorded. The Frisco cannonball stopped at the Springdale station on Sunday, October 17, 1897, to take on passengers, meeting a freight train pulling out of a siding at Lowell a few minutes later. The ensuing crash resulted in one of the worst wrecks this section had known. Two dead and five injured were extricated from the tangled mass of splintered cars and taken to the Arcade Hotel in Springdale.

On January 30, 1912, orphans were put on the famous Orphan Train in New York bound for northwest Arkansas. These children traveled on the Frisco and were placed in homes in Springdale and its vicinity. Originally, the rails crossed the highway south of town, but after a few fatalities at the crossing, the last during the paving of the new highway, an underpass was completed in 1935. At the peak of World War II, trains passing through Springdale consisted of 6 regularly scheduled passenger trains and between 20 and 25 freights each day, sometimes hauling as many as 350 cars.

Following incorporation of the city, one of the earliest concerns of city fathers and residents was that of good roads to connect to trade centers. The need was especially dire after the coming of the railroad when it became important that

45

farmers haul their produce to the city for shipment. Good roads meetings were held from time to time, where committees appointed to supervise road work and convict labor arranged to assist in the road work.

At one time, the principal work done on roads was that donated by people of the town and county. Those with enough money could buy the labor of someone else; otherwise, every able-bodied man was expected to give so many hours a month toward road improvement. Workers were often handicapped by a lack of equipment and machinery with which to work. Someone might offer the use of his mule teams, plows, or other farm tools for a specific amount of time. County assistance could be counted on to help improve the major rural thoroughfares. In 1904, both Emma Avenue and Holcomb Street were graveled. To handle heavier traffic, two steel bridges were built on roads leading to and from Springdale. In 1905, the Highway 45 bridge was completed and, in 1912, a bridge on Highway 68 East was built.

Before the advent of the automobile, livery stables ran a thriving business. Draymen found plenty of business hauling and delivering. In Springdale, Fate Stokes, P.A. Graham, and Sam Stokes all owned livery stables. H.A. Dailey owned a busy dray stable. Livery stables catered to young men, who hired rigs to call on young ladies. Picnics, celebrations, and box suppers in neighboring communities made heavy demands on the local stables. Rigs were reserved for regular customers who had arrangements at appointed times.

Dr. C.A. Smith was the first man in town to own an automobile, which he purchased on November 1, 1907. Able to go as fast as 25 miles per hour, it was a one-cylinder horseless carriage with 9-horsepower engine, a high seat, and a dashboard. The horrendous, noisy contraption created havoc as Smith drove down the street on his calls. Horses and teams snorted and plunged about, threatening life and limb of anyone unfortunate enough to be in the way.

It wasn't until 1910, when it became obvious that these horseless carriages weren't going away, that folks began to take the need of better roads seriously. Discussion turned to making improvements on Old Wire Road. Mayor Ownbey called a meeting and workers were assigned to each and every road leading into Springdale: Old Missouri Road, Old Wire Road, the roads leading to Lowell, Tontitown, Elm Springs, Butler, Huntsville-Spring Valley, Zion, and Fayetteville.

When a group of workers assembled at 7 a.m. on Wednesday, September 3, for the first big effort, the Springdale Merchants Band furnished music for the assemblage. By 8 a.m., workers had set out to go to work on the roads. Businessmen who were unable to work contributed cash, which was used to buy dynamite for blasting, lumber for bridges, and other needs. In 1924, Emma Avenue was paved through the business section.

U.S. Highway 71 originally followed the route of Old Missouri Road and ran the length of the business district along Emma Avenue. When the highway was paved in 1930, the route was changed to run west of town, keeping traffic out of the business area. The highway was opened on July 5, 1930, and Springdale celebrated with a two-day jubilee attended by Senator Joe T. Robinson. The

WAGONS LOADED WITH STEEL FOR CONSTRUCTION OF THE WHITE RIVER BRIDGE. It wasn't until 1910 that people realized the horseless carriage was not going away and saw a need for better roads and bridges. (Courtesy of D.D. Deaver and Shiloh Museum of Ozark History.)

dedication and celebration was attended by 16,000 people and Emma Avenue was closed for a big street dance. The paving of the highway made way for Springdale to become the hub of the fruit industry. Two years earlier, the *Springdale News* had used as its header, "Printed in the Heart of the Ozark Fruit Belt." If it hadn't been completely true then, it certainly was once the highway improvements were made.

Those improvements also opened the way for the expansion of businesses until they lined both sides of the new highway, sprawling north and south. By then, the town had spread almost to Elm Springs on the west and was quickly heading east as well. Much as downtown had shifted for the railroads, it did so again for the highway. Traffic soon clogged the thoroughfare and it was widened into four lanes. Improvements to the major route increased in importance and, through the years, a freeway or Interstate became a point of contention. U.S. 71 was a through-route from the Canadian border to New Orleans. As late as the 1970s, battles were waged over the widening of this north-south corridor. While no one, especially farmers in the area, wanted slabs of concrete in their backyards, many reluctantly agreed it might be the only solution.

Battles continued for several years over the route the highway would follow and whether it would be a toll road or freeway. By the 1980s, traffic congestion along Highway 71 from the Missouri border, through Springdale, and on to Fayetteville was horrendous, and the strip was often referred to as an endless parking lot. A bypass to the west eased the congestion somewhat. Finally, in 1989, construction

HIGHWAY 71 ROAD CONSTRUCTION SOUTH OF SPRINGDALE, 1913–1917. This road was once called the O.T. Trail. (Courtesy of Shiloh Museum of Ozark History.)

began on an interstate that would connect Fayetteville and Springdale, and effectively all of northwest Arkansas, to I-40 to the south. The projected date of completion was 1998.

The 540 Interstate through northwest Arkansas, connecting the busy area to I-40 down south, was opened in November 1999. Its route shifted the heavy truck traffic several miles to the west of Springdale and offered two exits to reach the growing metropolis. Highway 68 became highway 412, a busy east-west thoroughfare that cuts through Springdale and connects to Tulsa to the west. It is also the main exit from the interstate to downtown. Plans are now underway to build a 412 Bypass to alleviate some of the traffic jams.

It was inevitable that, with the earliest struggles to build better roads, someone would see the opportunity for successful and profitable over-the-road hauling of goods. With its heavy agriculture base, Springdale was destined to become a center for trucking that would spread far and wide. Some of those pioneers would make names for themselves across the country. None could be more well known than Jones Truck Lines, otherwise known as JTL.

In 1917, Harvey Jones went into the hauling business with a wagon and team of two mules, one red and one black. When he sold the wagon and mules, he used the profits to purchase his first truck. The year was 1919. He formally adopted the name Jones Transportation Company and, in 1933, the business became Jones Truck Lines. Later, Jones was awarded the Magnolia Agency for oil and gas, and found himself driving to Fayetteville to bring back his supplies. Since he was going anyway, he decided to haul goods there as well. Such a business grew steadily and, in 1927, he added more trucks to his line. By 1937, he operated 44 trucks out of the depot in the eastern part of town. The depot took up a city block and two more blocks were occupied by accessory buildings and the oil agency.

JTL was incorporated on October 22, 1934, with Harvey D. Jones, Taylor Jones, and Ulyss A. Lovell as incorporators. By 1937, the company's many loading docks, the washrack, blacksmith shop, lumber yard, and plumbing shop employed 80 to 90 men. A barber was employed on Sunday mornings and a barber chair was set up in the club rooms, which were fitted for his employees with pool tables, card tables, checkers, dominoes, papers and magazines, shower baths, lounges, and other conveniences. Jones had his own apartment at the plant and he had a strict creed that he followed: all purchases by the company were paid for in cash.

When trucking rules were made more stringent in 1925, Jones obtained a permit under the grandfather clause to operate anywhere in Missouri, Arkansas, Kansas, and Oklahoma. He was one of the first to file under the Inter-State Commerce Motor-Carriers Act of 1935. By 1949, JTL was one of the largest individually owned and operated truck lines in the country. In 1962, Jones owned 446 trailers serving Arkansas, Illinois, Indiana, Mississippi, Missouri, Oklahoma, Kansas, Tennessee, and Texas. These areas were served by 26 modern terminals.

Considered very civic-minded, Jones was chairman of the Springdale Memorial Hospital board of trustees, president of the Springdale school board, past president of the Springdale chamber of commerce, a member of the

ONE OF THE FIRST JONES TRUCK LINES TRUCKS, 1919. *In 1917, Harvey Jones went into an over-the-road hauling business with a wagon and two mules, one red and one black. (Courtesy of Jones Truck Lines and Shiloh Museum of Ozark History.)*

Joe Robinson's Trucking. This white, sleeper-type tractor was for over-the-road chicken hauling. (Courtesy of Joe Robinson and Shiloh Museum of Ozark History.)

Springdale Agricultural and Industrial Foundation, and the first president of the Springdale Benevolent Association. He was also president of the First National Bank, Frez-N-Stor, Incorporated, and of the corporate affiliates of JTL.

Another pioneer trucker was Joe Robinson, who came to Springdale in 1923 and began farming and raising poultry. In 1938, he branched off and began buying and selling fruits and vegetables out of the Clarkson building on the east side of Springdale. Robinson got into the trucking business in the early 1940s with two trucks. He hauled hay out of Oklahoma and just kept adding to what he would carry. He sold out his trucks after a son was killed in one of them. A new trucking business was started in 1945 with the construction of a new terminal. His trucks carried the first live load of poultry, delivering the chickens to California in trailers he built himself. Each carried 5,000 live birds. Robinson also helped develop the state lake at Elm Springs and was involved in the movement that resulted in the development of Beaver Lake as a water supply for northwest Arkansas.

There are no less than 26 truck lines, large and small, still operating out of Springdale today. Lindley Truck Lines was established in Springdale in the fall of 1933 by Lester Lindley with one truck. By 1937, he had 11 trucks. J.B. Hunt Trucking is headquartered in nearby Lowell, and Willis Shaw is based in Elm Springs on the outskirts of Springdale. Shaw began his firm in 1938 with one truck, which he used to carry live poultry from local growers to processing plants in Chicago. Willis Shaw Frozen Express is one of the top four refrigerated carriers in the country today. By the mid-1930s, Crown Coaches and Santa Fe Trailways Transportation also operated 22 buses daily through the town.

Taking to the air came naturally for many shippers of goods and produce. Bryan Work owned and flew the first airplane in Springdale. It was a 1930 model with a 3-cylinder, 30-horsepower Szkeley engine. Springdale's first airport was located at Stobaugh's farm east of town where the rodeo grounds are today. Owned and operated by a private corporation, the airport was obtained by the city in early 1950 for $25,000. An administration building was constructed that year at a cost of $10,000. Two expansions followed, one with the purchase of 17 acres in 1952, and another in 1958 with the purchase of 40 acres. In 1958, a new paved runway, 2,500 feet long, was completed with lights and paved taxi aprons at a cost of $50,000.

City fathers decided that the airport should be updated so that it could accommodate any twin engine executive-type aircraft and smaller commercial aircraft. In 1962, plans were completed to lengthen the runway to 3,000 feet of paved surface and extend the lights. The small airport is unique in that it is located entirely within the city limits, only one-half mile from downtown.

In April 1946, John Tyson received 2,000 chicks from Ray Ellis, manager of South Central Air Transport, flown into that airport. The day-old chicks were hatched in New Hampshire by the originator of the Hampshire Red Strain and shipped by air to Springdale. The pilot was R.H. Truax. This marked the first air shipment of poultry into the area, only a portent of what was yet to come.

Aerial View of the Springdale Municipal Airport, 1955. Obtained by the city in 1950 for $25,000, this unique airport is located in its entirety within the city limits of Springdale. (Courtesy of Raymond Ellis and Shiloh Museum of Ozark History.)

4. Build Us a City

The little two-room Frisco depot, lighted with kerosene lamps, was the magnet which drew the town's industries closer and gave to the newly developing fruit industry an impetus which has made Springdale one of the State's most important shipping points.
—*Springdale News*, 1937

Homesteaders had discovered the rich lands around and about the town and men looking for business opportunities arrived to begin various industries. Mostly through the efforts of Joseph Holcomb, the Washington County court issued orders of incorporation on April 1, 1878, and, not surprisingly, Holcomb was elected the first mayor on June 13, 1879. The first town aldermen were W.R. Ritter, C. Petross, J.B. Baggett, A.J. Hale, and R.M. Huffmaster. S.S. Purcell was the town's first recorder.

Holcomb became an early patron of education, employing a teacher to come at his own expense. He also organized the first Sunday school. A public school was conducted in a frame building near the Primitive Baptist Church. Baptists, Methodists, and Primitive Baptists all held services in the Primitive Baptist Church. The Masons used the second story as a lodge hall.

As owner of most of the town site, Holcomb laid out the property into city lots, which he sold and traded. He did what he could to energize new business to move to town. He gave away lots to those who would erect business houses and built the first brick building in town. He also donated land to public enterprises.

A wagon shop built in 1845 by John Holcombe, and destroyed during the Civil War, was rebuilt. E.T. Caudle operated a brickyard on South Holcomb Street. T.E. Flinn, Tom Roach, and a German named Ackerman had a tanyard and harness shop in town, and dealt also in home manufactured boots and shoes. In 1871, John B. Steele erected a general store in town. It was built of a fast and cheap construction called "box construction" without stud walls, which made it architecturally interesting and historically significant. The building would house the Springdale Post Office from 1877 through 1880 and be preserved as one of the very few remaining of a style once common in Arkansas.

Enormous changes were in the winds. Up to that time, the town business houses tended to cluster in a square around the little city park on Main Street.

James Blake Baggett (1842–1916). He was an early Shiloh blacksmith in the late 1860s through the early 1880s. His shop stood at the corner of Johnson and Main. (Courtesy of James P. Lichlyter and Shiloh Museum of Ozark History.)

Millard Berry and Dr. John Young made many trips by wagon to the White River to dig up small trees, hard maples, oaks, and others. They hauled them back and set them out in the park. James Baggett had a store there, near to Slaughter & Searcy, A.M. Phillips, and the Lovelady Stage and Inn Shop. The town well was located on the southwest corner of the square. Two blacksmith shops were located on the square, one across Church Street and another on the west side of Main. A store was built just south of the square on Main, but no one today knows to whom it belonged. The names James Baggett, an early blacksmith, and Searcy are often mentioned in connection with that store. When the town library was built in 1927, it was located on the old square. Shiloh Museum occupies the site today.

Near the intersection of Holcomb Street and Emma Avenue stood the town pump, which supplied the business section with water. The horses and mules that pulled the heavily laden wagons into town watered at Spring Creek, which cut directly across Emma Avenue. Over the years the creek had gouged deep gullies in the street so that pedestrians along the main thoroughfare had to climb down the banks and up on the other side. Later, a board footbridge was laid across the creek.

In 1883, there were only two buggies in the entire town and they were kept in the livery stable owned by Fate Stokes. The rest of the population went on foot, on horseback, or in wagons. Stokes stable, established by W.I. Stokes, was said to

EMMA AVENUE IN THE EARLY 1900S. An electric light hangs in the center of the street and poles can be seen along the left side. A sign on the trash receptacle reads, "We Lead!" (Courtesy of Shiloh Museum of Ozark History.)

be the first in town, but this would soon change. The *Springdale News* published the following in 1899:

> Bicycle riders should be careful when meeting buggies or vehicles on the public highway, especially if the occupants be ladies. Some horses that are perfectly sane in all other respects get stark crazy at sight of a bicycle and as a result there is a runaway. While this is true, it should also be remembered that the man on a bicycle has as much right to a share of the public highway as the man on the wagon.

Then there occurred an event that would forever change the town and the lives of its inhabitants. In 1881, after more than ten years of haggling, and through the efforts and pledges of many businessmen in both Springdale and Fayetteville, the St. Louis San Francisco Railroad announced that it would pass through both cities. With its coming, the original six lots John Holcombe had platted were given to Springdale.

The businesses clustered around the town square gradually moved toward the shiny new ribbon of tracks and Emma Avenue, not Main Street, became the central street of the town. Some villages in northwest Arkansas were faced with the task of moving long distances to be near a railroad. Springdale simply scooted their business district over a couple of blocks a little at a time. As if to cinch the permanency of the move, wooden sidewalks were installed between businesses in

1888. When the old town on Main Street moved to the new town on Emma Avenue, brick business houses replaced wooden structures.

An article in the *Springdale News,* dated January 24, 1967, quoted local historian Lockwood Searcy:

> A verbal reconstruction of the old square is almost impossible because information is both vague and conflicting . . . The square grounds became dormant and left to the wind as it grew high in weeds and grass. Sometimes a good citizen would hitch his team to the mower and cut the grass and weeds.

Though the old town was eventually deserted, Thomas G. Gladden continued to operate his hotel that provided accommodations for both man and beast. A recent map, drawn to depict Springdale in 1876, shows the Lovelady Stage and Inn Shop occupying an entire block between Center and Price Streets on Main. Originally built by Bennett Putman, from 1858 through 1861 the inn served travelers riding the Butterfield Stage, which passed a good mile away. The house

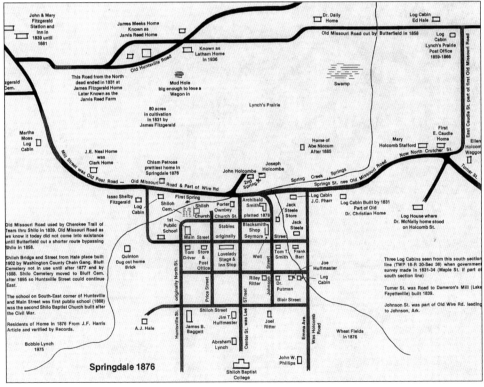

MAP OF SPRINGDALE IN 1876, DRAWN FOR THE CENTENNIAL OF 1978 BY BOBBIE LYNCH. *Local historian Lockwood Searcy stated that it was almost impossible to accurately recreate the original square because information was vague.*

had a good reputation for feeding its customers the very best meals and otherwise seeing to their comfort. So, the stage made the detour to take advantage of its facilities. This was the only stop through the Ozark portion of the route where passengers could comfortably rest and await the coming of the next stage, should they desire.

The two-story tavern had eight rooms with chimneys on either side, which served two fireplaces upstairs and two down. It survived the Civil War and, in 1885 or 1886, Gladden bought three-quarters of the tavern and moved it to the northeast corner of Center and Main. The other quarter was moved to property where Central School was later built and was occupied by the Lewis family. The remainder became the Gladden Hotel, often called the Springdale House, which served the Fisher stage line, not the Butterfield, which no longer existed. When the railroad arrived, Gladden used a one-horse spring wagon to meet trains to transport the baggage of drummers. The hotel was struck by lightning and burned to the ground on May 28, 1889. Gladden rebuilt the original hotel in 1893. Up until it was razed during urban renewal efforts of the early 1970s, a group of citizens hoped to restore the historic old hotel, but that never happened.

Gladden also built a three-story brick hotel in 1890 on Emma Avenue and called it the Arcade. However, many continued to refer to it as the Gladden, which creates further confusion concerning the Gladden's history. Photographs of the Arcade are often identified as the Gladden. A May 1951 issue of *Flashback*, published by the Washington County Historical Society, states that Gladden was the last to move from Old Town and he built the Arcade Hotel, a brick building,

GLADDEN HOTEL. *The building was rebuilt on the old square in 1893 and stood until urban renewal in the early 1970s. (Courtesy of Mrs. Willie Bryan Lindley and Shiloh Museum of Ozark History.)*

THE JAMES LEWIS WASHINGTON RESIDENCE. *A portion of the original Lovelady's Inn, it was divided in the 1880s. The other portion served as the Springdale House or Gladden Hotel until it burned in 1889. (Courtesy of Bobbie Lynch and Shiloh Museum of Ozark History.)*

ARCADE HOTEL. *This structure was built by Thomas Gladden in 1890 on Emma Avenue after the original Gladden Hotel burned. (Courtesy of Mrs. L.W. Searcy and Shiloh Museum of Ozark History.)*

FIRST APPLE FAIR IN SPRINGDALE. *The "Come to Springdale" sign is made of apples. (Courtesy of Shiloh Museum of Ozark History.)*

while other sources tell that it would be three years before he rebuilt the Gladden in old town, at which time it is surmised that he sold the Arcade.

Two other hotels were built in the 1880s to serve travelers on the railroad. The Frisco House, built in 1883 by Joseph Holcomb, was on the north side of Emma Avenue just east of the railroad depot. The other, the Commercial Hotel, built in the 1880s on the northeast corner of Holcomb and Meadow, was owned by William Stokes. It was also known as the Blue Goose Hotel. Besides bringing about an increase in construction, the arrival of the Frisco paved the way for an agricultural boom none could have imagined.

It is widely believed that the first apples to grow in the region were planted by the Osage, Choctaw, and Cherokee, but settlers soon saw that the climate and soil were perfect for orchards and began to plant seeds, then graft and grow many varieties. Visitors flocked into town to spend their money and enjoy this new prosperity. John H. Lichlyter, with his 80 acres of mixed crops southwest of town, was one of the sections' first farmers.

Hundreds of carloads of apples, strawberries, peaches, and grapes were eventually shipped out by rail. At such times, the entire town would turn out for festivals to honor the harvest of these fruits. An article in the 1937 *Springdale News* read:

> The little two-room Frisco depot, lighted with kerosene lamps, was the magnet which drew the town's industries closer and gave to the newly developing fruit industry an impetus which has made Springdale one of the State's most important shipping points.

J.F. Harris was born in Lawrence County, Missouri, in 1854. In 1886, he came with his family to a farm near Cave Springs. On his 20th birthday, he arrived in Springdale to continue his schooling and entered the school taught by Barnes and Adams in an old brick building that would one day become Central School. Two days after he entered school there, he helped carry the body of Grandma Holcombe, wife of the first Primitive Baptist pastor, Reverend John Holcombe, to her grave across the street from the church. He worked for J.B. Baggett in his blacksmith shop and hauled lumber for Chism Petross, one of the earliest businessmen of the settlement.

Harris was in the shipping business and served as city marshal for several years. His most colorful memory was the occasion of Springdale's bank robbery in 1901. Though he did not state in the interview what bank this was, it had to be either the Bank of Springdale or the Farmers and Merchants Bank, since these were the only two in existence at the time. After the robbery, he and Judge Millard Berry, with other citizens, searched the hills until they found the robber's hidden coat with bank notes stuffed in the pockets and recovered, in all, more than $3,000 of the bank's money. Returning to the bank, they told the cashier they wanted to make a deposit and laid the money before him.

Prior to 1868, banks were illegal in Arkansas and the county seat of Fayetteville had only had such an institution since 1871. In November of 1888, the Bank of Springdale was founded by Philip Wagoner, Amos Stealy, and H.A. Wagoner. In 1889, it was sold to local citizens. J.R. Harris was president and B.W. Bryan served

INTERIOR OF THE BANK OF SPRINGDALE, C. 1890. *From left to right are Millard Berry; J.P. Deaver; J.R. Harris, president; and Christopher Columbus "Kit" Phillips. (Courtesy of D.D. Deaver and Shiloh Museum of Ozark History.)*

as cashier. The Bank of Springdale was located in a small wooden building on West Emma.

Other banks would soon follow. First National Bank was founded in 1907 by Dr. C.G. Dodson and James Deaver. The partnership between Deaver and Dodson was formed in 1907 and they founded the First National Bank into which the Bank of Springdale was later absorbed.

Dodson arrived in Springdale as a young boy in 1879 and lived there until his death in 1929. Born in Lawrence County, Arkansas, on July 2, 1865, he was the son of Mr. and Mrs. Gibson Dodson. In 1866, he moved to Benton County with his parents and, in 1879, the family settled in Springdale. After studying dentistry under J.B. Dare and later at Vanderbilt University, he opened an office in Springdale, but his investments in business began to make such demands on his time that he gave up his practice to engage in other affairs.

Dodson's soon-to-be banking partner James P. Deaver was born in Elm Springs in 1855, educated at the University of Arkansas, and moved to Springdale in 1884. The following year, he married Emma B. Dupree, for whom Emma Avenue was named. Deaver was also identified with a number of business enterprises in the city.

After Dodson helped organize the First National Bank, he served as its first president. Actively connected with several Springdale business houses, he was a stockholder to many more, while owning a great deal of real estate in the city and surrounding country. He was a commissioner for the construction of the

Drawing of First National Bank, Founded in 1907. After the Bank of Springdale merged with the First National Bank, it was robbed in October 1931. Four unmasked men escaped into Cookson Hills with $5,000. (Courtesy of May Reed Markley and Shiloh Museum of Ozark History.)

EMMA DEAVER, WIFE OF JAMES P. DEAVER. Emma Avenue was named after her. (Courtesy of Shiloh Museum of Ozark History.)

municipal water and sewer system and was largely responsible for the Welch Grape Juice Plant that located in town in 1925.

In 1894, the Farmers and Merchants Bank was organized. The First State Bank was founded in 1923. In 1932, the First National Bank and the Farmers and Merchants Bank merged and retained the First National Bank name. In later years, other banks would come to town, but these formed the financial foundation on which the city would grow into the late 1950s.

With the arrival of new industry, Holcomb saw a need for a newspaper and induced Oswald C. Ludwig to come from Alabama and begin the publication of Springdale's first, *The Enterprise*. Ludwig came to Springdale in 1880 from Alabama and established the newspaper in a small frame building on Holcomb Street. *The Enterprise* was a small sheet that contained little news, but was liberally patronized by advertisers. There, as a young boy, John P. Stafford worked as printer's devil (an apprentice).

In 1885, H.C. Warner, formerly associated with the *Arkansas Traveler* in Little Rock, came to town and began publication of *The Yellow Jacket*, a four-page, four-column paper. The plant was sold after some months to G.C. White, who moved it to West Fork where he published *The Republican*. For a while, Price Brothers

JOHN P. STAFFORD. *At the age of 18, he became the editor of the* Springdale News. *(Courtesy of Shiloh Museum of Ozark History.)*

published the *Springdale Journal*, but then moved to Fayetteville. In 1885, B.Y. Hunt published the *Springdale Gleaner* with Millard Berry as editor. They took over the Price Brothers plant and leased it to Damon Clark of Bentonville, who, in 1886, changed the name to the *Springdale News*. After a few months, H.M. and J. Van Butler purchased the printing plant and began publication of *The Springdale Locomotive*. H.M. Van Butler left shortly after to found a paper in Prairie Grove and, in May 1887, J. Van Butler sold the plant to John P. Stafford for $275.

John Pleasant Stafford was born December 4, 1868, the son of John N. and Mary Holcombe Stafford, and a grandson of Pleasant and Margaret Reed Stafford, who came to Washington County before 1856. When he was only a year old, in 1869, John N. Stafford was killed by bushwhackers. In 1884, he went to work on the *Fayetteville Democrat* and, in May of 1887, he purchased *The Springdale Locomotive*, one of the many newspapers that had served the growing town. May 7, 1887, marked the birth of the *Springdale News*.

At 18 years of age, Stafford is said to have been the youngest newspaper publisher in Arkansas. A few fonts of type, a cheap job press, and an "army" press on which the paper was printed were all set up in a 14-foot square room in a downtown frame building. Flickering oil lamps lit that first newspaper office. The circulation of the weekly, six-column, four-page paper in the first year was 182.

Among the first advertisers was Holcomb, who owned and operated the Frisco House near the depot on Main Street. A typewriter was installed in 1890 and, for one week that year, the newspaper was published every day, before going back to a weekly publication. During the Spanish-American War, which began in 1898, the newspaper was published daily for several days beginning May 3, in order to provide the latest telegraph news of the war.

In the 1890s, patent medicines were the main source of advertisement income for country newspapers. Some advertisers of the day were Paine's Celery Compound, Herbine, Dr. Harter's Iron Tonic, Tujtt's Pills, Swamp Root, Wine of Cardui, Dr. Miles' Heart Cure, Hood's Sarsaparilla, Piso's Cure for Consumption, Ozmanlia Oriental Pills, Dr. Moffett's Teethina, and Early Risers Easy Pills. Stafford found it difficult to collect what was owed him in ad money and for subscriptions and decided it might be wise to barter. After that, subscribers sometimes paid for the paper by hauling a load of wood to the office to heat the building.

The most popular feature of his newspaper was the country correspondents, who sent in news from outlying communities, such as Johnson, Spring Valley, Elm Springs, Oak Grove, Goshen, Harmon, Sonora, and many others. News writers and reporters included Marion Murphy, Marlon Mason, James A. Venable, H. Myrick, J.T. Sturdivant, Miss Willis Hayes, Roy Reed, Ernest Wilburn, Mrs. H.E. Tooker, Mrs. E.S. Holland, Mrs. D.I. Gallaher, and T.C. and Maudine Sanders.

OFFICE OF THE SPRINGDALE NEWS, JUNE 1910. In its first year of operation, the weekly newspaper had a circulation of 182 and was printed in a 14-foot-square room. (Courtesy of Maudine Sanders and Shiloh Museum of Ozark History.)

In March 1903, after several moves, the *News* was settled in a building erected by Stafford on Emma Avenue. He experimented with a twice-weekly paper in 1904 and again in 1909, but it wasn't until July 1928 that he went to twice a week every week. The header on the newspaper read, "Printed in the Heart of the Ozark Fruit Belt."

In 1888, Stafford married Lena Southwick Claypool. The couple had four children. She passed away in 1902 and, in 1904, Stafford married Marion Murphy and they had three children. Besides managing the successful newspaper, Stafford spent much of his time in the service of his community. He served as secretary of the Springdale Savings and Investment Club in 1888. In 1891, he helped organize the Springdale Baseball Association and was a member of the city band.

In 1902, Stafford was elected to the state legislature and served two terms. In 1929, he was president of the Arkansas Press Association. Stafford passed away on September 24, 1933. All of his seven children had done duty at the newspaper at one time or another. One of his sons, Guy, would later become mayor of Springdale; another, Edward (Marty), became the editor of the newspaper upon the death of his father. Like their father, his children took an active part in civic duties for the betterment of their community.

In 1904, Springdale became the home of a man who would one day become a state senator. Wilson Cardwell was a descendant of pioneers who came to Fayetteville in the early 1800s. He was born in Zion, Arkansas, in 1868. Growing up, he worked on his father's farms and was one of the first local growers of strawberries for commercial purposes. He married Quilla May Boyd in 1887 and

POSTCARD SHOWING APPLE HARVEST. *By 1887, the J.B. Gill nursery was shipping thousands of trees for planting and Springdale fruit was regularly taking top prizes in fruit fairs all over the country. (Courtesy of Mrs. L.W. Searcy and Shiloh Museum of Ozark History.)*

they had eight children. Cardwell came to the city in 1904 to give his children educational advantages and bought a small farm north of town. He was an apple salesman for Brogdon & Company and, for 13 years, was a salesman for the Southern Berry Growers' Association, which he helped to incorporate. He always believed that strawberries were the best crop grown in the region. On the advice of friends, Cardwell ran for the state legislature and, in 1913, was elected to his first term. He was elected again in 1917, 1923, 1927, 1929, 1931, and was elected to the state senate for a four-year term in 1933.

The Welch Grape Juice Plant came to Springdale on November 25, 1922. There was a parade to the site and speeches made by C.W. Pool; J.F. Welch, vice president of the company; and W.F.D. Batjer, president of the Rogers Community Club. Wilson Cardwell was in charge of laying the cornerstone.

Many other prominent citizens contributed to the growth of Springdale in those years after the war. They built businesses and served the city truly and well, adding to its prosperity. A.E. Smyer was born at Newton, North Carolina, in 1853. He was the son of Mr. and Mrs. Logan Smyer. In 1871, he came to Arkansas and settled at Hindsville. He married Marta Ann Cline in 1873. In 1886, he went in business with his son to operate the New York Store in Springdale. He retired in 1921, then served as justice of the peace and later as collector for the Springdale water and sewer districts.

Though there were many thriving businesses, it was farming, and especially the growing of fruit, that led the town to its greatest prosperity prior to World War II. Carl A. Ownbey was a prominent farmer, fruit grower, and businessman. Born near Springdale in 1879, he was the son of Mr. and Mrs. Julian Ownbey and a brother of the well-known Colonel W.G. Ownbey, who would make his mark serving his country. In 1903, Carl Ownbey married Beulah Jones of Westville, Oklahoma, and they had several children. For many years, he served as an active vice president of the Farmers and Merchants Bank. He was also chairman of the 1926 grape festival.

One of the first men to engage in fruit growing for commercial purposes, and a pioneer of the northwest Arkansas fruit industry, was W.B. Brogdon. Born in Trenton, Tennessee, in 1854, after the Civil War, Brogdon went to Texas and engaged in the mercantile business. In 1880, he married Dee Jackson of Corsicana, Texas, and came with her to the city in 1888. When he arrived, he planted an apple orchard and, when he later sold the land, he planted another large orchard. The Arkansas State Horticultural Society owes its reorganization largely to Brogdon's efforts, and he served for some time as its president. He was an eager contributor of time and money in the interest of the betterment of the community.

Schooled at Cane Hill College, George W. Kennan came with his family to Springdale in February 1881 and took up the nursery business until 1883. He was born in 1861 in Strickler where his father kept a stagecoach stand. Kennan didn't remain in the nursery business long. He soon apprenticed with Tom Hughes of Evansville, who had set up a photograph gallery and watch, clock, and jewelry repair business. In August 1886, he was furnished a stock of jewelry by the late J.L. Duke

Haxton Woolen Mill. This building was located on the east bank of Spring Creek on Mill Street. (Courtesy of Shiloh Museum of Ozark History.)

of Duke Jewelry Company of Fayetteville. That same year, he bought a lot for $50 and built a small building for his business. His business moved several times over the years, but always remained in Springdale. In January 1887, he married Ella N. Cannon, daughter of William and Fannie Cannon of Evansville, Indiana.

As the town grew and prospered, many other businesses began that would serve the community well during its growth. The Springdale Woolen Mills (Haxton's), for example, was one of the city's claims of note for 30 years. In the first year after the city was incorporated, Mayor Jo Holcomb and other citizens induced the owners of a woolen mill at Wager in Benton County to come to town. The owners of the mill were W.B. Haxton, his son S.N. Haxton, and his son-in-law J.A. Armstrong.

Myrtle Umbaugh, daughter of S.N. Haxton, said that a shortage of water at the mill's original location contributed greatly to the decision to move to Springdale. Completed in 1879, the frame structure that measured 40 feet by 70 feet was two stories high with a two-story ell that was 18 feet by 24 feet. Workers did custom carding and spinning, and manufactured piece goods such as janes, lindseys, knitting yarns, blankets, and other goods. They operated 11 looms, 4 sets of cards, and 440 spindles. During the busy season, 14 workers were employed. The mill was the only one of its kind in the state.

In those days, many people raised sheep and produced their own wool, which they would take to the mill, making an outing of the trip. They would camp while waiting for their goods. S.N. Haxton also furnished all the woolen fabrics for the public institutions of the Cherokee Nation. Myrtle Umbaugh recalled that the Native Americans came to Springdale to purchase blankets and fabrics and, in addition, her father made trips to Indian Territory to sell the products of the mill.

The mill kept two wagons busy on the road taking orders and selling piece goods while they did custom work. Haxton's was a boon to the city not only because of the increase in trade, but because quality woolen goods were supplied to the townspeople at low prices over a period of many years. When the mill was torn down in 1908, it had not been in operation for over two years.

The Springdale Roller Mill was also located on Mill Street. It thrived in a day when all the flour used in Fort Smith came from the mills of Washington County. Built in 1881 by Chism Petross and J.R. Harris, it milled most of the wheat grown in northwest Arkansas. By 1888, the mill was producing 100 barrels of flour per day. L.D. Petross, a brother of the founder, was manager of the mill for 30 years. Both corn and wheat were turned into high-grade flour, choice table meal, bran, and feed. One product, self-rising flour, sold under the trade name of Springdale's Best. The roller mill was the only one of its kind in the region. Fire destroyed the structure on March 5, 1921, and it was never rebuilt.

A man who is credited with bringing to Springdale more than a hundred families was real estate entrepreneur Joseph S. Ewalt. He was born in Lewis County, Missouri, in 1864 and married Clara Diffenbacher of Great Bend, Kansas. In 1904, he moved from Great Bend to Alma and later to Springdale. He operated the Springdale Roller Mill after the retirement of L.D. Petross. Under his management, the mill did $100,000 worth of business a year. Ewalt also served as mayor for two terms, and it was largely through his efforts that the municipal water and sewer plant was built.

In 1887, the town council purchased 12 lampposts and set them up at strategic points about the town. Uncle Dick Lichlyter was town marshal at that time and it

MILL STREET TO THE NORTH WITH SPRING CREEK IN THE FOREGROUND. *The building is the Petross Flour Mill, the largest roller mill in several states. A buggy is fording the creek. (Courtesy of Bobbie Lynch and Shiloh Museum of Ozark History.)*

fell his lot to be town lamplighter. The marshal was also expected to enforce the law, collect dog taxes, and collect occupation license fees. He was assisted by a night watchman. Also in 1887, with mud 8 inches deep in the streets, Tolbert Lane was named chairman of a committee to procure sidewalks and, in February, the first sidewalk was built from the business section of town as far as the school building.

A wish list was published in the newspaper in 1890:

> *The News* would like to see: The cemetery cleaned up; everybody prosper and be happy; some sidewalks built; a $15,000 hotel built; a good wagon factory; our public school liberally patronized; more people come here to live; real estate take a boom; a good fruit evaporator; farmers come to town to trade; the merchants advertise more than they do; a hook and ladder company; a good pork packing establishment; people with money to invest locate here; a good old fashioned religious revival in this town; 300 new subscribers enrolled on our books by January 1st; 50 new residences built in the next year; the people unite in a grand effort to boom the town; less drunkenness and cutting up on our streets, especially on the Sabbath; young people conduct themselves in a more becoming manner when they attend church; some of those old frame buildings on Emma Avenue torn out and substantial brick ones built in their places.

A WAGON AND HORSE AUCTION, 1909. The auctioneer is in the wagon with his hand raised. Future mayor Tolbert Lane is the man with his jacket open in front of the auctioneer. Former mayor L. Dallas Petross is partially behind the horse's nose. Other identifications are tentative. (Courtesy of Shiloh Museum of Ozark History.)

CHAIN GANG BUILDING SHILOH STREET BRIDGE OVER SPRING CREEK, C. 1902. Since the county and town had no funds for such work, county prisoners were often used for road work and bridge building. (Courtesy of Mrs. Braun and Shiloh Museum of Ozark History.)

Some of these improvements were sorely needed.

County prisoners were customarily used for road and bridge construction since the county and towns had almost no funds for such work. In 1902, such a chain gang built the Shiloh Street bridge over the creek. The cry for prohibition grew with the town and the Woman's Christian Temperance Union became vocal in its opposition to the sale of liquor and, in particular, the state's new native wine law, which permitted the manufacture and sale of wine made from local grapes and fruits.

In June 1901, every business closed down on Sundays for the first time in observance of the new Arkansas Sunday closing law, often referred to as the "Blue" law. It would restrict businesses far into the twentieth century before being repealed.

Smallpox in March of 1898 forced Springdale to be quarantined against Fort Smith because of the disease running rampant in that Arkansas River Valley settlement to the south. A business directory for the year 1900 stated that the city had a population of 2,000. It included in its listing five physicians, a dentist, two banks, a newspaper, two hotels, and numerous grocers, general stores, meat, produce, and fruit stores. Industry had a hold as well, with the woolen mill, a canning company, and a manufacturing company. No mention was made in this listing of the four evaporators or the important roller mill. By 1904, there were 2,500 people, two lumber yards, a planing mill, four evaporators, and the only

AUDITORIUM AND CHAUTAUQUA GROUNDS. The auditorium was built in the fall of 1904 specifically for this popular event and torn down in 1932 when its popularity waned. (Courtesy of Mrs. L. Searcy and Shiloh Museum of Ozark History.)

woolen mill in the state. A single cannery employed 100 to 200 hands. That year also produced a bumper crop of tomatoes, apples, strawberries, and grapes.

C.F. Renner wrote in *Fruit and Farm Magazine,* in 1904, that Springdale had the following:

> nine churches, eight secret societies, a Confederate Veteran Camp, an annual Chautauqua Assembly which furnishes each year the best talent the country affords, the State School of Seventh Day Adventists—and we don't have saloons, negroes, mosquitoes, malaria, chills, bawdy houses or other vices of this nature.

Land was worth $20 to $150 an acre, depending on improvements. Ladies could buy extra-heavy, ribbed seamless cotton hose for 20¢ and a cloak with a shoulder cape for $3.50. Gentlemen might adorn themselves with oil grain standard screw bottom shoes at the modest price of $1.65.

An unpopular curfew law attracted ridicule, as it stated that no person under 20 years of age could be on the streets of town after 9 p.m. The streets were so muddy in the spring of that year that the children could not go to school. Civic agencies of town agitated for lights and waterworks, as well as a cold storage system. The colt shows at Ownbey track east of town were the big events of

Saturday afternoon and the chautauqua was the high point of the summer. The local stage aspirants tried out their luck at the Opera House and played to packed houses. Ice cream suppers were in vogue as benefits for the band and baseball club.

The year of 1904 proved to be an active one in the growing community in many respects. That year, the following item appeared in the newspaper:

> The Bank of Springdale has purchased an adding machine which works with human-like intelligence. The longest column of figures can be printed and the total given by simply pressing a lever and pulling the crank. It cost $375, and *The News* will manage to run its business a while longer without investing in one of them.

In 1907, voters approved a measure to extend the city limits, increasing the population by about 500 people. On April 19, 1907, three automobiles, all owned by Fayetteville men, created a great to-do as they rattled through the streets of Springdale. Properly impressed, Springdale doctor C.A. Smith took receipt of the first automobile in town. By 1911, 25 automobiles roamed the streets.

Dogs and chickens continued to wander the town freely, as did a number of milk cows kept by town folks. In 1907, voters decided to prohibit town cows from wandering the streets. The Anti-Horse-Thief Association was very popular and its members were active in their efforts to stop all stealing of horses, cattle, hogs, or any livestock or property. Their familiar sign, a red and black horse and rider inside a horseshoe with the words "Protected by A.H.T.A.," stood near many farms and residences. Another popular organization was the Woodmen of the World. Formed by an insurance company by the same name, it supported adults' clubs, as well as boys' and girls' clubs, that taught carving and catered to woodworkers.

In 1911, a sign was erected outside Springdale that contained the following message:

> What Springdale Has: 2500 population; 50 business houses; 2 good schools; 8 churches; 1 meat market and cold storage; 1 canning factory; 1 planing mill; 1 sawmill; 2 livery barns; 2 lumber yards; 3 banks; 2 vinegar factories; 1 auditorium; 3 RFD routes; 1 flouring mill; Largest fruit evaporator in the US; Excellent Climate; Good water; Pure mountain air.

Despite being plagued by storms—some of tornadic proportion—floods, droughts, and fires, the city survived and continued to grow. One of its most destructive fires occurred in the business section on Tuesday, January 12, 1915. The conflagration caused a loss to the downtown area of $25,000, a goodly sum in those days. A flood on January 26, 1916, closed down the power plant, dismissed school because of a flooded basement, and poured water into stores on the south side of Emma.

OZARK POULTRY AND EGG. Poultry was an exceedingly lucrative trade for Springdale. This company was a forerunner of Jerpe Company, Swanson and Sons, Campbell Soup, and Gregory Center. (Courtesy of Ann Sugg and Shiloh Museum of Ozark History.)

The region has always suffered from an erratic winter climate, with warm gulf breezes one day, blue northers the next, occasionally both in the same day, as on February 2, 1917, when the temperature dropped from 61 degrees to -2 degrees in a matter of hours. On January 10, 1918, 14 inches of snow fell in an area that normally experiences less than that in an entire winter. This was the heaviest snowfall since February 1886. The following day, January 11, the temperature was -11 degrees.

A man who would prove that hard times were no match for grit and fortitude, Harvard Harp began his career in 1924 at City Mercantile, a dry goods store. Harp was born and raised in Springdale and is responsible for creating a chain of grocery stores that have expanded into three states. His father, a farmer, died when Harp was 13 years old. After working in the citrus industry in California, he returned to Springdale with his wife, $500 cash, and the desire to open a grocery store. In 1930, he set up Harp's Cash Grocery at the corner of East Emma Avenue and Water Street. Harp made his own deliveries in a truck with the store name and phone number hand-lettered on the door. Starting a successful business at the height of the depression, Harp proved that hard times wouldn't hurt a grocery business.

In its Golden Anniversary issue in 1937, the *Springdale News* reported glowingly of the city:

> The Legion Hut is a community center, clubs and church organizations provide an outlet for the constructive energies of a progressive and

public-spirited population and the canneries, shipping houses and evaporators draw to Springdale the fruit trade of a wide area. The shopping center of the town is modern and attractive. Truck lines, bus lines and the railroad, with its seven daily trains, provide all types of transportation. One/fifth of the apples of Arkansas are marketed from here. The huge Welch Grape Juice Plant and Nelson Wineries offer a ready market for grapes. The vinegar factory is one of the town's important assets.

Farming and poultry raising bring a vast amount of trade into town. Poultry raising now ranks as one of the leading industries of the locality, and the land hereabouts is well adapted to truck farming. The tomato crop is among the most important single crop of the county.

Once the terrible years of World War II were over, Springdale mushroomed as it never had before, building on the foundation laid by those early industrious entrepreneurs, some of whom would become well known throughout the entire country.

NELSON WINERY AND DISTILLERY. Built next to the Nelson Canning Factory and incorporated in 1933, the winery distilled 200,000 gallons of wine yearly. (Courtesy of William "Bill" G. Nelson and Shiloh Museum of Ozark History.)

5. Serving the People

The story of the mails, of the bringing of messages through wild country and bleak weather to anxious men and women in the faraway corners of the earth has always been a colorful story and one in which romance is blended with practicality. Not less so is the story of the postal service of Springdale.

—*Springdale News*, 1937

Communication with the outside world was hard to come by for the growing town. There was postal service of a sort to the county seat of Fayetteville as early as 1829, but residents of Springdale had to go there to pick up their mail. In 1834, a petition was presented to Congress by 182 persons asking for a mail route to begin at the Crawford County Courthouse approximately 50 miles to the south and ending at Springfield, Missouri. The route would go through Mulberry, Russel's in White Oak, Hilburn's on the headwaters of the White River, Fayetteville and Osage Springs, then south of Bentonville. It followed a very early trail used by both Native Americans and white settlers and shown on an early survey map of 1830 to 1834.

Though this improved mail service, Springdale residents still had to pick up their mail in Fayetteville and the situation remained that way until the government contracted John Butterfield to establish his overland stage and mail service in 1858. Within a year, he had built 141 stations for the new mail company. The station at Fitzgerald's was built of native stone and still stands northeast of Springdale on the Old Missouri Road near its intersection with Wire Road. It is not known if Fitzgerald built it as a stable for his inn or if it was built by Butterfield to replace an earlier log stable.

Butterfield used existing roads wherever they met his purposes, but built new ones when they did not. He decided not to use the part of Old Missouri Road that ran through Shiloh along what is now Mill and South Crutcher Streets and Caudle Avenue. That decision must have disappointed city residents, who had hoped the stage would go through town, but they made the most of it when he cut a more direct road from Fitzgerald's Inn to the point where Caudle and Highway 265 intersect today, effectively bypassing Shiloh.

Fitzgerald's was not a post office, though, and it was another year before Lynch's Prairie Post Office was established in a little log cabin located on what is

FITZGERALD STAGE COACH STOP ON OLD WIRE ROAD. The natural rock structure stands today, but the inn itself, one of the first buildings in the area, is gone. (Courtesy of Shiloh Museum of Ozark History.)

now Caudle Street and Old Missouri Road. Not downtown, precisely, but certainly closer than Fayetteville. Records indicate that the cabin was one of the first in the area built by J. and Deborah Lynch shortly after 1830 on the E.E. Hale Farm. A.O. Gregg owned the Hale farm, so when postal service was established there in 1859, he became the first postmaster and put up a small store. He operated both on the road east of town.

Local mail service came to a halt during the Civil War. Residents went back to picking up their mail in Fayetteville. Even before incorporation, it became evident that the biblical name chosen for the town by its founder would have to be changed. Since the demise of the Butterfield Line before the Civil War, delivery of mail was sporadic if not totally nonexistent. In May 1872, representatives of 28 families and 5 businesses petitioned the government for a post office and learned there was already a post office at Shiloh in Van Buren County. A new name must be found.

Many possibilities were discussed at a town meeting, including Holcombtown, Huffmaster, and Putmanville. Sarah Reed Meek, the wife of James Meek, one of the town fathers, mentioned to her husband that the settlement was a beautiful spring-in-the-dale. The name was shortened and officially adopted. Credit is sometimes given to Meek's daughter, Nannie Reed Bench, but family descendants give Sarah the credit. The community, resplendent with its new name, continued to thrive.

Once the name of Springdale was settled on, townspeople had themselves their first post office. Historian Bobbie Lynch says that the first post office was located in B.F. Putman's home, located on what is now the southwest corner of Blair Street and Johnson Avenue. In 1876, it was moved to William H. Lovelady's store and he became postmaster. In those days, this was common. Convenience counted for a lot and, often, the postmaster was a local storekeeper. It wasn't unusual for folks to show up at the post office, only to find its location had been moved. This happened again in 1877 when it was moved to the John B. Steele store on the south side of Johnson Avenue. Christopher Columbus "Kit" Phillips served as postmaster.

Until the coming of the railroad in 1881, mail continued to arrive by stagecoach on the U.E. and E.L. Fisher Stage Lines, which made a circle from Fayetteville north to Springdale, then by circuitous route to Pierce City, Missouri, and another route south via Neosho, through Bentonville and on to Fayetteville. The passenger fare from Fayetteville to Pierce City was $16.

There was no individual mail delivery. Everyone went to the post office to pick up their mail, though probably not every day. Men would gather waiting for the arrival of the stagecoach. It was more of an event than the later custom of waiting for the arrival of the train. When the mail was unloaded, the postmaster would open the bags and read aloud the names of those receiving mail.

The first rural mail route was established on August 15, 1900. Patrons weren't required to put up regulation boxes and the mail was left in a variety of containers from stove pipes to dry goods boxes. Carrier W.M. Sweeney carried the mail in

POST OFFICE, 1908. *In early days, patrons went daily to the post office to pick up their mail, but in August 1900, the first rural mail delivery was established. (Courtesy of Thelma McKinney and Shiloh Museum of Ozark History.)*

two cigar boxes for quite a while on the route, but by 1904, he had 158 boxes to carry. By 1912, there were three rural routes and three star routes carried on a contract basis and not under civil service. Sam Stokes was contractor for those routes and carried the mail by hack. By 1937, five rural routes, more than 1,000 boxes with a combined mileage of 227 miles, were being served. By May 1, 1937, when Springdale had grown to a population of 3,500, a new federal post office was constructed at a cost of $65,000. It was considered to be one of the most attractive federal buildings in northwest Arkansas.

C.J. Chapman was the first mayor to draw a salary. The year was 1890. As yet, there was no fire department, no city water supply, and no electric lights or telephones, but Springdale was poised on the threshold of a new era. Ten years away from the new century, its citizens struggled to turn the growing settlement into a city. To do that, certain services must be made available beyond churches and schools.

As it turned out, one of the churches would establish what would one day grow into a public library. Prior to that, John Stafford, editor of the *Springdale News*, had a lending library at the newspaper office. The cost was 10¢ per week. After a while, he sold the books to W.G. Ownbey, who loaned them out from his drug store. In 1888, W.Y. Winton had established a circulating library with dues of $1 a year. There weren't many books, but all proved that the citizenry was ready for a real library.

Reverend W.G. Brandstetter, pastor of Central Presbyterian Church conducted a daily vacation Bible school in the basement of the church. Books were donated by members of the church and a bookshelf opened to church and Sunday school members. Interest in the church library grew and Mrs. Inez McFee was asked to help organize it. She agreed on the stipulation that it be open to the public. A board of trustees was formed and a president named. The library was organized to meet the standards of the American Library Association.

By September of 1923, about 500 books had been donated, but the library still had its quarters in the church basement. Volunteers catalogued the books, and sufficient funds to purchase 100 additional books were donated by the Sunday school and other friends of the project. The first librarian was Mrs. J.W. Johnson. The library was conducted as a free circulation library open three afternoons a week. Teas, dinners, and entertainment were held to provide funds for its maintenance and growth. Besides holding a local talent chautauqua, the library sponsored a hamburger stand at the grape festivals and other entertainments, including Mrs. Jarley's Wax Works, which proved a profitable enterprise. At the end of the first year, more than 1,500 books were catalogued and donations were increasing. Clearly, more room was needed.

In 1926, the library constitution was revised to conform with the articles of incorporation adopted by the library board and placed in the hands of Judge Berry. The library was incorporated with a self-sustaining board in February and the task of finding a permanent home was undertaken. The first building funds drive brought in $3,000 in cash and pledges. Permission to build the library was secured from the city. In the spring of 1927, construction began and, on August 28 of that year, the building was dedicated. By 1937, the library contained 4,000 books and subscribed to 30 magazines

In November 1940, the library board voted to accept Works Progress Administration (WPA) supervision of the library. Mrs. Mattie Neal was employed as librarian. Mrs. Letha Brogdon, who later served for many years as Springdale's city clerk, was hired as assistant librarian at $10 a month. Washington County quorum court appropriated funds for a county library in 1940. In September 1941, the Springdale library became part of the Washington County Library System. In 1948, a general election voted on a one-mill tax for the county library and the first funds were received in 1950. Books were purchased for the county library and distributed among the libraries and schools in the county.

In the late 1800s, several bad fires in town had prompted the formation of a volunteer fire department. In 1887, a fire caused the destruction of the fruit evaporator owned by Jo Holcomb. Citizens fought the blaze, which threatened nearby residences, with a bucket brigade. On May 28, 1889, the Gladden Hotel was struck by lightning and burned to the ground. People staying there were roused in time to escape without injury, but guests did lose their clothing to the blaze. Proprietor Thomas Gladden suffered a $7,000 loss. The *News* headlined the event as "The Fire Fiend" and within the article stated that the city desperately needed a hook-and-ladder company.

After C.A. Jones' wood shop caught fire in 1891, a proposal was made in the *News* for the organization of a hook-and-ladder company with the following humorous suggestions:

> We suggest A.J. Hale as captain and James Welton first lieutenant. As members we want first Jeff Lewis, he is selected for his thoughtfulness in washing out the buckets before taking the water to the fire. Greely Vinson should hold the nozzle for he put water on everything in sight, including John Hazelwood who was out of sight. Charley Chandler comes next from the fact that he would not lose any of the appurtenances of the machine, this act was made evident when he set his bucket down to go after the pencil he had dropped.

The first hook-and-ladder company was organized in 1891 with A.J. Hale as captain and James Welton as first lieutenant. The company had little equipment, but luckily, the town had no serious fires for the next nine years, although on March 4, 1894, Stone's Livery Barn burned. With no fires to fight, interest waned for a couple of years, but the department was quickly reorganized in 1893 with Mayor Chapman as chairman, Theo Parker as secretary, H.G. Hunt as fire captain, and C.G. Dodson as lieutenant.

On September 24, 1901, the Springdale Hotel burned. Flames were spotted at 1 a.m., and the two-story frame building burned to the ground in 30 minutes. Aroused by the firing of pistols and the ringing of church bells, everyone formed a bucket brigade to carry water from the town branch. The entire business district was threatened. Both Sanders Grocery and Farrar Hardware caught fire several times. A week later, the Kimmons Walker and Company Fruit Evaporator, the largest such business in Arkansas, caught fire and burned to the ground. At peak harvest season, 50 employees processed 1,000 bushels of fruit per day. C.J. Chapman's evaporator was destroyed by fire in September of 1905.

Bucket brigades and a hand-drawn chemical wagon were all the equipment those first volunteer firemen had to work with. None of the early, ill-equipped organizations could be termed a success, but on September 6, 1909, the Springdale Volunteer Fire Department Number 1 was organized. Meeting first in the old light plant, the group elected C.L. Smyer as its first fire chief, Millard Lear as first captain, and J.P. Bennett as secretary-treasurer. Membership was limited to 30 men between the ages of 18 and 45. Initially, 19 men joined

After the reorganization of the fire department, a new method of summoning firefighters was adapted when a fire whistle was installed in February of 1910. The whistle was 4 feet long and 10 inches in diameter. It wasn't too long before the fire department was called into action by that whistle. The Frisco Hotel experienced a rash of fires soon after the fire department's reorganization and a blaze destroyed the nine-room residence of Mrs. M.E. Umbaugh.

Despite the highest of hopes for a modern department, from the beginning the organization suffered from a lack of working materials. Had a truly disastrous fire broken out at that point, firemen could have done little except let it burn. The

SPRINGDALE PUBLIC LIBRARY, 1944. *In 1927, construction began on the first actual library building and, in 1937, it boasted 4,000 books and subscriptions to 30 magazines. (Courtesy of Shiloh Museum of Ozark History.)*

SPRINGDALE FIRE TRUCK NUMBER 1. *From left to right, the men are Millard Means, Bill Lear, Andrew Ballew, Zack Curry, Earl Simonds, Ernest Umbaugh, Glen Simes, Everett Head, and Joe Nix. (Courtesy of* Springdale News *and Shiloh Museum of Ozark History.)*

situation had to be remedied, so C.L. Smyer, F.B. Young, and J.P. Bennett were appointed to raise funds to purchase ladders, pails, and other equipment. Some of the first fund-raisers were in the form of plays and entertainments offered by the men in the department. These were surprisingly successful and a few were deemed utterly delightful by patrons, who attended the productions held in the auditorium. These, in turn, led to trips to surrounding towns where they presented their popular plays and minstrels. The firemen soon made a name for themselves in the entertainment field. In 1912, the first chemical equipment, a small hand-drawn chemical wagon, was secured with funds raised by these performances.

In January 1915, the department faced its biggest fire to date when Brodie's photo studio caught fire at 1:40 a.m. and threatened the entire business district. Over the years, other fires damaged various businesses downtown. The New York Store, Umbaugh Brothers, the C.H. Hewitt Building, and the G.A. Graves building were all damaged at one time or another by fire. On March 5, 1921, fire destroyed the landmark Springdale Milling Company (Old Roller Mill), erected in 1881 by C. Petross. In July of 1922, the old Phillips residence, another landmark believed to be the oldest house in town, burned.

In 1917, the first motorized truck was purchased, a three-quarter-ton Republic on which ladders were mounted. Though any could drive it, the honor usually went to Zack Curry. There was a dispute about the purchase of a fire truck for which firefighters had raised $265. The men threatened to resign unless the city bought a truck, so the council finally gave in and bought a Federal fire truck for $5,400. A combination hose and chemical truck, it was christened "Number One." Further fund-raising allowed the purchase of 1,000 feet of hose.

The Ladies Auxiliary was formed on February 11, 1928, with Mrs. Andrew Ballew serving as its first president. Twelve charter members met in the room above the fire truck storage room until 1932 when they moved into the basement of city hall. Each member brought some kitchen utensil or convenience to the first meeting.

A La France 500-gallon pumper arrived in 1931 and became Number Two, at which time the company felt prosperous enough to donate the old Republic to the water department. The city donated quarters in the basement of city hall for the fire department's weekly meetings in 1932. On alternate meeting nights, the volunteers worked at laying hose, raising ladders, and learning the duties each held on the squad.

In 1937, a new Chevrolet chassis truck with a long wheelbase and dual wheels went into service. The hose rack from the old Federal truck was used on the new truck, which was also equipped with a booster pump, increasing its efficiency for small fires and fires away from the large water mains. A.M. Ballew, elected fire chief in 1920, still held that position in 1937. The department had 15 regular members and 4 extra. One paid full-time fireman was on duty.

One reason early fires destroyed so much property was the lack of available water. In 1907, the city had water service, but only for about a year. The first water tower was 90 feet high, a wooden tank with a capacity of less than 10,000 gallons. A gasoline engine, with a pumping capacity of 100 gallons-per-minute, supplied water from Holcomb Spring to eight to ten users who paid whatever they were able for the service, which only lasted a year. It wasn't until 1921 that a contract was let to drill deep wells. By December of that year, Springdale had a brand new water system and a dry well, abandoned at 500 feet. In 1922, the city bought 20 acres near Stultz Spring from which water would be secured for the municipal water system. Five years later, the line to the pump station was enlarged and a modern filtering plant installed.

The early equipment of the municipal water supply consisted of two pumps and a chlorinator. The chlorinator had to be switched from one pump to another, but one day in 1927, someone forgot to switch the chlorine feed. The omission was not noticed for about three days. Within a couple of weeks, Springdale had an outbreak of typhoid fever. Following that near catastrophe, bonds were issued to build a settling basin and a filtration plant along with a clear well for chlorine treatment. In 1928, improvements made possible by a $50,000 bond issue brought the city plenty of pure water from the springs. One septic tank was installed at that time and another was put in in 1935. By 1937, there were 562 consumers in service, with the water supply still coming from Shiloh and Fulbright Springs, which also serviced 76 fire hydrants. An adequate sewer system was installed in 1947.

The one man responsible for the arrival of telephone service to the city was Millard Berry. He was born in Davis County, Indiana in 1856, and there he practiced law for a while. In 1878, he married Ida McIIolland and, the following year, went with his wife and parents to Dallas County, Texas, where his mother's health soon demanded a change in climate. The family came to Springdale by way of the Choctaw Nation in 1883, traveling by wagon and buggy and spending three weeks on the road. They rented a house on the lot where Berry later built a home. When he first arrived, the old town had just been moved onto Emma Avenue and he had no intention of staying. Berry formed a partnership with John R. Harris shortly after his arrival and sold farm machinery. After a year, he made a contract with a wagon company at Leavenworth, Kansas, and, for two years, traveled through Texas selling wagons to the retail trade. Captivated by the town, its hospitable people and the many business opportunities, he opened an abstract office and settled down to stay.

For a time, Berry was connected with the Springdale Manufacturers Association, which made furniture and installed the city's first water works. During the first year of Berry's term as judge, he succeeded in having a three-mill tax levied to provide a building fund to replace the old Washington County courthouse, which was a 60-foot square brick building in the center of the Fayetteville square. The new courthouse was designed by Charles Thompson of Little Rock and was completed in 1904.

An article in the 1937 *Springdale News* Golden Anniversary Edition reported the following:

> Up in Judge Millard Berry's house there is a piece of polished brown wood, hollowed here, curved there, fitted with a bit of fabric, a length of wire and a brass button. It looks like the beginning of an electric table lamp, but it isn't, it is the beginning of a telephone system.
>
> In the days before "Central" was summoned by the lifting of a receiver and any voice on the continent was at the bidding of Springdale, this queer contraption used to be Springdale's first telephone. There was another just like it, and a length of copper wire a quarter of a mile long ran from one to the other.
>
> One of these so called queer contraptions was at the Springdale Roller Mill and the other uptown at B.P. Deaver's store. It was used because the store handled the roller mill's accounts. When communication was needed, one would tap on it with a lead pencil, which would set up vibrations which were amplified and transmitted through the vibrating brass button and the copper wire and the men at the store talked to the thing. It worked on much the same principal as the tin can telephones used by youngsters.
>
> Judge Berry swore it worked, but the reporter writing the article wondered if perhaps folks at the mill might not have stepped out their door and shouted "Answer your acoustic telephone."

JUDGE MILLARD BERRY, 1908. Responsible for bringing telephone service to the city, as a judge, Berry also succeeded in providing a building fund to replace the old Washington County courthouse in Fayetteville. (Courtesy of Washington County Plat Book and Shiloh Museum of Ozark History.)

That was one story. Another states that in the spring of 1896, Judge Berry got tired of walking home on errands and bought two telephones from the Dunlap Construction Company in Springfield, Missouri. He put one in his home and the other in the Berry abstract office in the rear of the Bank of Springdale. Though he didn't intend to let town residents in on his new convenience, people kept dropping into the office and being fascinated by the strange product that he handled so casually. They wanted to talk in it too, but there was little point in that, since the other end was at his home. Had he not lived so far from his abstract office, Springdale might not have acquired electric telephones when it did

It wasn't long before Berry gave in to the pressure from so many curious folks dropping by to use the newfangled contraption and installed a five-drop switchboard. He probably regretted it immediately, for he had to be the operator when he was at the office and there wasn't any operator when he wasn't there.

The little switchboard formed the first connecting link for some of the businesses in town. After only a few weeks, five phones were not enough and the switchboard was traded in on a larger one with 25 drops. Charles Sanders was employed as operator. Then, a 50-drop switchboard replaced the smaller one and, at last, Judge Berry felt he had the telephone situation securely in hand. But once a modern convenience is introduced, there's no stopping the demand, as if folks hadn't gotten along quite well all those years without a phone.

The judge also had an abstract office in Fayetteville and driving back and forth soon became as tiresome as walking to his home and back. Fayetteville had a telephone exchange with a switchboard in the old First National Bank Building, so the Berry lines began to edge down the highway toward Fayetteville. The posts reached the city limits, but Fayetteville interests protested against the new line coming in. After a session with the city council and the Fayetteville Telephone Exchange, permission was granted and Judge Berry's line was connected to their switchboard. Now Springdale was connected to the county seat in a way it never had been before.

When the switchboard outgrew Judge Berry's office, it was moved upstairs with Fred Horton as operator. In 1899, J.N. Hulsey and Henry Cowan were lineman. Soon, lines were run to Rogers, then Bentonville, and from there, the line eventually crossed the border into Seligman, Missouri. Folks in Springdale began to realize how big a world was out there. After lines were strung east to Huntsville, the North Arkansas Telephone Company was formed with Judge Berry as president, James W. Dupree as vice president, J.P. Deaver as secretary, and acting treasurers G.G. Dodson and S.H. Slaughter. The company had a capital stock of $25,000. It made use of full metallic copper circuits with phones good for a 500-mile circuit.

In 1899, North Arkansas Telephone Company published an article in the *News* extolling the virtues of having a telephone in one's home. It ended with, "put one

CALVIN HOLCOMB HOME LOCATED BETWEEN SPRINGDALE AND ELM SPRINGS. *This home is typical of those in the city during the late 1800s. (Courtesy of Dorothy Haxton Scroggins and Shiloh Museum of Ozark History.)*

in your home or business house and after using it a short while it will prove such a convenience that you will wonder how you did without it."

Phone rates were raised from $2 to $2.75 a month in May of 1919. Eventually, the lines joined down south at Alma with the Bell Telephone system, which bought out the North Arkansas Company in 1915 and has operated the system ever since. In 1939, the company installed a dial system, but dialing for long distance calls wasn't initiated until 1969.

About the same time that Judge Berry began his struggle to install those first telephones, the city was engaged in a struggle to obtain electricity. Back in 1896, when Springdale was lighted with kerosene lamps and the town marshal made the rounds each evening to light the dozen or so lamp posts in the city, a man came to town prepared to put in electric lights, but influential citizens said no. They thought a better deal could be found elsewhere. As a result, nothing was done. Springdale citizens continued to make do with the glow of candles and lamps, while all around, towns came to life with electricity. It was not until the early 1900s that the city gave a franchise to United Power, Cold Storage and Electric Company, which proposed to build a cold storage plant for apples and to erect and operate an electric power plant. When the company failed to act, Spencer Owen and Associates was granted a franchise and given six months. Still nothing happened.

It seemed the city was doomed to darkness, but, in the winter of 1907, two young men from Cleveland, Ohio, came to town. M. Clyde Martin and Glenn C. Martin located their engine and dynamos in a brick building at the northwest corner of the auditorium grounds and put up an addition 20 to 40 feet east of the building for the boiler. The engine was capable of producing 90 to 130 horsepower and the boiler was 100 horsepower. The plant could furnish current for 2,000 16-candle power lights. The town's first electric light plant, known as the Springdale Light and Power Company, was in business. At long last, the city had electric lighting.

With no less than four lights installed in any residence, customers were billed 30¢ per month per 16-candle power light. For business houses, the rate was 60¢ per month for each light. The company ran lines to the outside of the houses and owners paid for inside wiring at the cost of material and labor. Immediately, the town contracted for street lights amounting to $45 per month. Three arc lights were placed in the business section and 32-candle power incandescent lights were used in the residential section. When the plant first opened, the service ran from dusk to 11:30 p.m.

The first lights in Springdale were turned on on April 1, 1908, and the Martin brothers held an open house at the plant. The grounds were lighted with incandescent lamps and an arc light was mounted on the roof, spreading a halo over the entire city. Nearly everybody in town went to the plant, as the owners showed their guests through and explained to them the workings of the system.

In 1915, the Martin brothers sold their plant to the Todd brothers. That company, with J.D. Trimble as plant engineer, operated the service until it closed down in September 1916 for lack of funds. Under the new management, the plant had been in frequent financial difficulties. Plus, high water in the plant during the previous winter caused considerable damage to the large generator. This, with other troubles, combined to make it impossible for the owners to continue the service with their limited capital. In February 1916, as flood waters engulfed the town, the lights went out, embracing citizens in an eerie darkness. For a week they waited, wondered if the lights would ever come back on. The dynamos and generators were submerged and the fire box filled with water. All the equipment had to be sent to Joplin to be dried. The disaster was described in the *News*:

> Shortly before nine o'clock the water in the lake began rising and the engines and generators were operated while the workmen stood in water . . . A warning signal was sent out from the plant a little after nine, and the lights were turned off, while the main drive to the generator was shifted from the large Corliss engine to the emergency engine. . .
>
> The water began rising very fast, and suddenly with a roar and a crash broke over and around the retaining wall and rushed waist deep into the boiler and engine room of the plant. Workmen at the plant . . . were able to carry out only their books and a few minor articles, all the machinery, tools, etc., being left at the mercy of the flood.

J.D. Trimble said he swam through the plant and rescued some of the record books from the desk.

Local business houses, creditors of the power and light company, issued a number of garnishments during the summer of 1916 and, when the plant ran out of coal, the owners were unable to obtain another shipment. Local merchants subscribed to a fund to buy coal and, eventually, the city took charge and advanced a sum of money sufficient to keep the plant going until the difficulties could be straightened out.

In September 1916, Springdale awoke one morning to find that their light plant operators had absconded with the advanced running expenses and left for an unknown destination. Clyde Martin, one of the former owners, who still held a mortgage on the place, took charge as receiver pro tem. The following month, the Martin brothers re-assumed complete control of the plant and soon installed a 24-hour service. At long last, after a summer fraught with high water and intermittent darkness, the city could once again light its streets, businesses, and homes.

In the summer of 1917, the Martin brothers sold their plant to the Middle West Gas and Electric Company of New York. At first, the plant at Fayetteville, which was owned by the same New York company, supplied Springdale with current, but later, a high tension line was built to Springdale and a sub-station established. At that time, the city had about 325 consumers. In 1928, the Southwestern Gas and Electric Company of Shreveport bought the plant, together with all the Arkansas holdings of the company.

Uncle Jack Trimble, who began his services for the Springdale Power and Light Company in 1913 under its original owners, the Martin brothers, said that when he came to work at the light plant, there were only 24 meters in use in town. The plant was operated by an 80-horsepower Morris slide valve engine with a 60-KVA generator and one boiler of 13-pound pressure capacity. Direct current was used until the purchase of the plant by the Southwest Power Company, when an alternating current system was put into use.

In 1937, power was obtained from Welekah, Oklahoma, through the central distributing point of the Oklahoma Public Service Company of Tulsa. The substation, built in 1930, "has the most modern equipment obtainable, including a remote control system by which the main line switch can be turned on and off from Fayetteville by telephone." Southwestern Gas and Electric Company became Southwestern Electric Power Company (SWEPCO), which serves the city today.

Ozarks Electric, a consumer-owned utility, was incorporated in 1938 to provide electric service for member-consumers over a wide area of rural northwest Arkansas and eastern Oklahoma. The utility built 3,115 miles of line through the rugged, nearly inaccessible hills to serve 12,984 families and businesses in parts of nine counties in Arkansas and Oklahoma. As late as the 1950s, lines were still being installed in remote rural parts of the county that had never been served with power.

RICHARD M. LICHLYTER AND FAMILY. Lichlyter is seated with wife Sally; standing, left to right, are Josie Lichlyter Johnson and sister. A rural family, the Lichlyters owned one of the area's first farms and grew fruit on 80 acres of land. (Courtesy of Mary Ellen Johnson and Shiloh Museum of Ozark History.)

First attempts to provide a hospital for city residents did not come about until 1908 when the Sanitarium & Hospital was founded by George Kerr and his wife, who had served in Africa as missionary nurses. Dr. Frank Young treated his patients there and performed surgery. The hospital was located in a building of 14 rooms directly behind the old Haxton Woolen Mill. It was originally the home of Mrs. S.N. Haxton and had been built in the style of the Gladden Hotel, with porches upstairs and down halfway around the house.

In 1909, the *News* stated that the hospital had received 48 patients and had 11 operations since its opening. People were treated for typhoid fever and residents were also given turkish baths. On the lush lawns of the hospital, tents were erected, producing the appearance of a great circus or safari, for in those days it was believed that good, clean air had a curative value. Unfortunately, the hospital had a short lifespan and closed in 1910, probably because City Hospital in Fayetteville was being built.

Dr. C.P. Sisco had a small ten-bed facility in the late 1920s in his upstairs office, which was in operation for about ten years. Patients were sometimes kept for as long as three days with Carrie McFadden, his nurse, caring for them.

It wasn't until 1948 that physicians and others started a concerted effort to fund a hospital. Cake sales, pie suppers, and pledges raised $200,000. An additional $400,000 was acquired through the Hill Burton Act, which matched federal funds two-to-one with local funds. A 32-bed, T-shaped hospital was opened on Quandt Avenue in 1952. Within two years, another campaign was held to build a needed

SPRINGDALE MEMORIAL HOSPITAL OPENING CEREMONY, SEPTEMBER 1952. *Some 2,000 persons toured the 32-bed, $600,000 building. (Courtesy of Springdale Memorial Hospital and Shiloh Museum of Ozark History.)*

FIRST MEDICAL STAFF OF MEMORIAL HOSPITAL, 1952. From left to right are the following: (front row) Dr. J.W. Dorman, Dr. Friedman Sisco, Dr. C.S. Applegate, and Dr. P.L. Hathcock Sr.; (middle row) Dr. Charles F. Bloom, Dr. Ralph Weddington, Dr. Ed Wheat, Dr. Preston Brogdon, Dr. Coy Kaylor, and Dr. Lawrence H. Siegel; (back row) Dr. Anthony DePalma, Dr. Fount Richardson, Dr. Jim Stocker (dark shirt), Dr. Max McAllister, Dr. Joe Bill Hall, Dr. Harrison Butler, Dr. Fred Ogden, Dr. Jim Mashburn, and Dr. R.H. Huntington. (Courtesy of Shiloh Museum of Ozark History.)

wing across the back. Some of the earliest doctors to practice in the area prior to and after the hospital opened were Dr. Friedman Sisco; Dr. J.W. Dorman; Dr. Stanley Applegate; and Dr. A.J. Harrison. The Hospital Auxiliary was founded in 1952 by a World War I army nurse, Eva Atwood. Its members provided more than 40 services to the patients. The hospital was later expanded to a capacity of 210 beds.

Springdale has always been blessed with an abundance of service organizations. A forerunner to its influential chamber of commerce was formed in January of 1904. Known as the Commercial and Improvement Club, it was aimed at the organization of businessmen for betterment of civic conditions, with street improvement and market centers being two chief objectives. Unfortunately, nothing much came of the idea and it was soon discontinued.

In August 1920, the Community Club was organized. Its purpose was to promote the interests and welfare of Springdale and the community. Perhaps the time was right, or maybe those who organized it were more attuned to the wishes and needs of the community, or it was simply an idea whose time had come, but the idea was a success. The Community Club was open to businessmen and women but also to fruit growers and others not strictly classed as businessmen. It was a principal booster for the waterworks and sewer system installed in 1922.

The ladies auxiliary to the club developed into the Civic Club, which remains one of the most active community organizations in the city. The Civic Club used its influence to begin the project for improvement of Highway 68 (now 412) between Tontitown and Siloam Springs. The work was completed in 1936 through the cooperation of the chambers of commerce of both Springdale and Siloam Springs.

The most outstanding accomplishments of the Community Club were the presentation and management of two grape festivals, which drew thousands of visitors to Springdale and gave the city the greatest publicity it has ever received. It also sponsored Springdale's participation in the annual Northwest Arkansas Apple Blossom festival held at Rogers. In the spring of 1930, the Community Club was officially reorganized into the Springdale Chamber of Commerce.

Some of its accomplishments over the years include distribution of loan applications and applications for government sale of drought-stricken cattle; sending delegations to Washington, D.C. for the purpose of securing a grape code for the benefit of fruit growers; furnishing information on spraying and other problems of moment to farmers and horticulturists; sponsoring innumerable civic projects of all kinds; and working ceaselessly for highway improvements.

The lighted athletic field and softball league were sponsored by the chamber, and, in 1960, it was largely responsible for Springdale coming in first in Arkansas in the community achievement competition among towns in the population category of 5,000 to 20,000. In 1962, a new site was purchased for a home for the chamber of commerce on Emma Avenue.

Ingrained in those first settlers was the desire to help others and from this came an abundance of civic organizations designed to do just that. The oldest of these is the Rotary Club, organized in 1925. The first one to be launched after World War II was the Kiwanis Club. The Bluff Cemetery organization came into being in 1905 and cared for the historical burial grounds. Daily, many selfless volunteers continue to see to the needs of the busy community.

6. Returns for Their Labor

Taking all things into consideration is it any wonder that the people of this vicinity are prosperous? What matters it to them in Wall Street? What care they if the frenzied financiers of the East fall afoul of each other and fight to a finish? Why should they trouble over the schemes of the politicians, or worry as to what will be the issues in the next campaign? So long as God sends the sunshine and the rain, things which no man can corner or monopolize, they are assured bountiful returns for their labor, and prosperity and happiness for themselves and those dependent upon them.

Great is Arkansas and great is Washington County, in which is the good town of Springdale!

—*Springdale News*, 1907

The first apple trees that would one day spread into acres and acres of orchards are believed to have arrived as seeds carried in by early immigrants from Kentucky and Tennessee. It is also thought that the Native Americans planted apples here earlier than that. Raised from seedlings, the trees produced many varieties, often named by the grower.

Before the coming of the railroad in 1881, vendors hauled their produce in wagons to southern and western markets. Production continued to increase until the great drought of 1901 placed a great demand on the apple producers of northwest Arkansas, which had escaped the arid conditions being experienced elsewhere in the country. Spraying had not yet begun, so the cost of production was kept low. Springdale enjoyed the advantage of gateways to Dallas and Fort Worth to the south; Memphis and Birmingham to the southeast; St. Louis to the north and east; and Kansas City to the north and west, making shipping an important and profitable by-product of the apple industry.

Chandler and J.F. Harris, Harris and Deaver, W.A. Claypool, and Brogdon and Son were among the first shippers. The men most responsible for the development of the city as a growing and shipping center for fruits of all kinds were G.S. Bouton, W.B. Brogdon, E.B. Littlefield, J.A. Eicher, D.E. Eicher, A.H. Glass, E.M. Bowden, L. Marks, Ward Lane, and James Welton. J.F. Harris was the Harris of the firm that had a thriving business as early as the 1880s. Will Claypool was connected with Chandler and Harris for two years before he went into the

Wagons loaded with Apples on Way to Sryer. The Arcade Hotel is in the background. (Courtesy of Freddie Fink collection and Shiloh Museum of Ozark History.)

shipping business for himself in 1904 and built a warehouse near the Frisco tracks. D.E. Eicher arrived in town in 1904 and, in 1910, became president of the Arkansas State Horticultural Society. In 1915, he was appointed assistant horticultural agent of the Frisco Railroad, assuming the post of agent in 1919.

In the fall of 1886, the first fruit show was presented in town. The Frisco ran excursions from the north and south, and thousands of visitors attended the two-day affair. Shown at the first fruit festival were Arkansas Blacks, Winesaps, Mammoth Blacktwigs, Northern Spy, Ben Davis, Autumn Strawberry, and Huntsmans' Favorite. Arkansas Blacks and Shannons were among the first varieties of apples commercially grown here, though neither retained its original popularity. Ben Davis was for many years a popular variety and was planted in great quantities throughout northwest Arkansas.

By 1887, the J.B. Gill Nursery was shipping thousands of trees each month during the planting season. Springdale fruit took prizes at fairs all over the country. Gill served as secretary of the Fruit Growers and Shippers Association during its early years. One of the first local organizations for the benefit of growers was the Northwest Arkansas Horticultural Society, with W.J. Todd, John P. Stafford, and W.G. Vincenheller among the early officers.

The first State Fruit Fair, known as the Horticultural Fair or Apple Show, was held in the city in 1894. Besides 100 varieties of apples on display, the A.D. Baggett farm exhibited two varieties of wheat, white and yellow corn, sorghum, sweet and Irish potatoes, pumpkins, hay, oats, blue grass, millet, rye, clover, peas, turnips, peppers, radishes, onions, and cucumbers, all of first quality.

Other businesses exhibiting were the Springdale Woolen Factory, Springdale Hardware and Implement Company, S.W. Clark Furniture Store, Springdale Canning Company, Walker and Walker, Lynn and Duncan, Graves and Son, Mrs. Watts, Mrs. Walker, A.A. Bartlett, Gabbert and Hunt, and the *Springdale News*.

After the drought of 1901, this area began to be noticed as an apple-producing region. In 1905, there were more fruit trees in Washington and Benton Counties than in any other two counties in the United States. In the spring of 1907, wagons loaded with strawberries filled the roads leading to the railroad depot where 100 train carloads were filled for shipment. Warmed and fed by rain and sunshine, the peach crop flourished and grateful farmers hauled and shipped 20 carloads. Then came the apple crop, the biggest ever known. Not only did farmers supply local factories with all their needs, a total of 400 carloads of the luscious fruit were shipped out that fall. Single pickings from some orchards brought as much as $15,000. From 1904 to 1924, the community regularly produced a 1,000-car apple crop. Occasionally, the worst would happen. In the spring of 1921, apple growers suffered two severe freezes that wiped out the apple crop for that season.

Judge Irvin Rothrock kept a man working for him the entire year at the prevailing wage of the day, and when the man picked enough apples for Anna Rothrock to bake an apple pie that fall, Rothrock joked, "That apple pie cost me $5,000."

Other fruits found much success in the region as well. Though never as bountiful as apples, the delicious Arkansas strawberries soon gained plenty of

MORE THAN 25 WAGONS LOADED WITH APPLES. *These wagons are lined up at C. Jones Brothers & Company. (Courtesy of Lichlyter collection and Shiloh Museum of Ozark History.)*

notoriety. In the spring of 1886, E.S. Horton began growing berries on one-seventh of an acre and, by 1889, was harvesting more than $225 worth of berries. By 1905, 2,500 acres had been planted in and near Springdale and 15 railroad cars were loaded out in one day.

As early as 1889, W.B. Brogdon and Son grew, bought, and sold not only the popular apples, but peaches, cherries, grapes, and strawberries. Their first farm at Eicher Corner at the junction of Highways 68 and 71 consisted of 70 acres in growing fruits. Come spring, as far as the eye could see were spread banks of snowy strawberry blooms. Clouds of pink and white blossoms in apple and peach orchards filled the air with a heady fragrance. Brogdon farms averaged a crop of 25,000 bushels a year over a 25-year period. In 1908, they bought 140 acres 2 miles northwest of the city, and by 1937 they were the oldest producing fruit firm still in operation.

In August 2, 1907, a newspaper editorial proclaimed that Springdale, or that portion of Arkansas known as the fruit belt, was in the midst of a season of prosperity unprecedented in the history of the state. Following the greatest strawberry crop ever known, there came the raspberry, blackberry, dewberry, and the early vegetables, which were high in production. And now the beautiful Elberta peach was also in high production, while waiting in the wings was the big Ben Davis apple, king of them all.

In 1907, one farm having 586 fruit trees netted the owner $2,121 for the apple crop. On another, 5,200 crates of peaches were gathered, netting $7,592. From a

PEACH PICKERS AT SPRINGDALE, 1910. *The peach crop in northwest Arkansas never reached the production of the apple crop because of warm early springs and late frosts that nipped the blossoms. (Courtesy of Shiloh Museum of Ozark History.)*

Packing Peaches at Brogdon Farm, 1915. The child in front is Dean Brogdon. (Courtesy of Springdale News, *Martha Brogdon, and Shiloh Museum of Ozark History.)*

Apple Harvest at Brogdon Farm, 1915. Brogdon and Son was among the first shippers of apples and was one of the businesses responsible for the city becoming a shipping center for fruits of all kinds. (Courtesy of Springdale News *and Shiloh Museum of Ozark History.)*

SPRINGDALE CANNING COMPANY, 1908. *The two-story brick building has an attached metal-roofed building. In the background, facing the road, is the vinegar factory. (Courtesy of Bobbie Lynch and Shiloh Museum of Ozark History.)*

10-by-15-mile area around Springdale, more fruit was shipped than from any other town in the state. The peach crop in Arkansas never reached the production of the apple crop. Early warm springs, followed by late freezes, invariably nipped the blossoms and destroyed entire crops.

W.H. Browning experimented profitably with peach growing and C.N. Miller had an orchard. The first orchards were started about 1900, but late freezes continued to prevent peaches from being a sure crop each year. However, in the years when they harvested a crop, the growers received a nice return on their investment.

In the spring of 1912, budded peaches were killed by a -12-degree freeze on January 12. Yet, in the following year, growers enjoyed the greatest peach crop ever known with 75 cars shipped the first week of August. By August 15, the total had reached 150 cars. That same year, 200 cars of apples were shipped. At the end of the highly profitable fruit growing season of 1911, the *Springdale News* published a special edition; it reported that 120 railroad cars of apples were shipped and unusually large quantities of apples were also used by local evaporators and vinegar plants. Kimmons, Walker and Company Evaporator used 100 railroad cars of apples; Southern Fruit Product consumed 71 cars for vinegar; C.J. Chapman and Company Evaporator used 60 cars.

In later years, careful spraying and incessant vigilance became necessary to protect apple orchards against the blights, insect pests, and other dangers that menaced them. The University of Arkansas maintained a moth hatchery in the college of agriculture. There codling moths were grown under such conditions as those found in orchards of the vicinity and when they developed to the danger point, the growers of the section were notified at once. Five long rings on a party line was the signal that summoned farm owners from their other work with the imperative message, "apply cover spray immediately."

This deadly little insect, which would one day effectively destroy most of the local commercial apple orchards, didn't make its appearance in the area until the trees were widely and well established after the turn of the century. Ruth Holt Payne wrote about the use of the moth lantern in fighting the destructive codling moth:

> Acres now dotted with broiler houses were once fragrant with apple blossoms in the spring, and the streets of the railroad towns were lined with wagons loaded with sacks of dried apples in the fall. The industry . . . still exists, to a limited extent—so does the battle with the codling moth, mother of the apple worm.

Payne described the moth lantern as an ordinary lantern hung in the trees at night, with a bucket of oily water placed beneath it. Insects flying against the hot globe fell to the oily water, where they were finished off.

Around the year 1914, farmers began to use the hand sprayer, 1 pound of dry lead arsenate to 50 gallons of water in a barrel to which a cylinder about 10 inches in diameter was connected by a hose. It was operated by a hand pump from the bed of a wagon. One man was required to work the pump, another to hold the spray hose on the tree, and a water boy to supply more water as it was needed. At least three sprayings were required: once when the blooms were in the pink bud stage, again when the petals were falling, and again about three weeks later.

Since the fruit and canning industry have always been closely intertwined, the canning factory was one of the earliest successful enterprises in the growing city. Pressure canning methods were unknown and only peaches, apples, tomatoes, and other products that could be easily preserved were canned. Packing was slow because each can only had a small opening in the top which, after it was filled, was sealed with a soldering iron. The capacity was only 3,000 cans a day.

In 1886, Millard Berry and other interested citizens formed the Springdale Canning Company and set up a small cannery in a two-story frame building east of the Frisco tracks. Some 40 residents bought stock in the factory. By October of 1887, the cannery offered employment to 100 people and packed 30 carloads of vegetables and fruits each season. In 1888, owners of the factory bought another lot and increased its capacity to 10,000 cans a day. Some 40 residents bought stock in the canning factory established on East Emma Avenue.

In 1918, J.O. Nelson and his wife established a three-line canning factory. That fall, they moved their location and, in 1933, built "the best equipped canning factory in Northwest Arkansas." Spinach, beans, tomatoes, peaches, tomato juice, and grape juice were canned.

It was not unusual to see small canning factories on large farms. A prosperous farmer would build a small canning shed, buy cans and pressure canners, and employ neighborhood labor, usually women and girls. He would operate only during the tomato or apple season. Many women found this employment a good way to add to their family's income.

Joe M. Steele operated the Steele Canning Company, with headquarters in Springdale, and canning factories in Lowell and Steele from 1923. Begun in a small 20-foot by 40-foot shed on his farm 2.5 miles south of Tontitown, by the 1960s, the company was the largest in Arkansas. He began by packing tomatoes during the summer months while attending the University of Arkansas. He found such a demand for his products that he soon devoted his full time to the canning industry. In 1932, the business outgrew the small plant and moved to Springdale. Steele and his cousin Luther E. Johnson joined forces in 1935 to found a canning industry under the name of Steele Cannery and expanded operations rapidly until the Depression. In 1937, Steele shipped the first trainload of canned foods ever shipped in the United States. This 28-car train shipment was publicized throughout the country as a first in the canning industry.

In 1938, Steele became the first customer in United States to ever buy a straight trainload of fertilizer at one time when he purchased it for the crops in the area. During World War II, the greater part of Steele's products went to the armed forces to help feed the boys on every battlefront. Steele again gained national

JOE M. STEELE. He founded Steele Canning Company and was president of Ozark Canners and Freezers Association from 1947 to 1948. (Courtesy of Shiloh Museum of Ozark History.)

KIMMONS WALKER EVAPORATOR COMPANY, KNOWN AS THE LARGEST IN THE UNITED STATES. Wagons loaded with apples to dry are lined up. (Courtesy of Austin Cravens, W. Fay Atkisson collection, and Shiloh Museum of Ozark History.)

recognition after the war when he received the "A" flag award for essential service in time of war. The continued growth of the factory was a major factor in building Springdale and northwest Arkansas.

Heekin Can Company, a major industry founded in 1901 in Cincinnati, Ohio, moved to town in 1948. Charles and Robert Smith built the first fruit evaporator with Kimmons and Walker, their close successors. The Smith Evaporator was called the largest in Arkansas, even before 1887. It was located near the Frisco depot. Two square towers, each three stories high, were known as Alden towers, and could dry up to 350 bushels of apples a day. The ground floor contained a large furnace and above this ran moving trays or screens drawn upward in a shaft by endless chains. The cut fruit was placed on the trays and a tray was inserted every half hour, passing upward through the shaft and emptied out at the top floor.

Kimmons and Walker bought the evaporator in 1904 and tore down the towers, rebuilding the plant. The evaporator worked on a different principle. The buildings were of wood and three kilns, 20 feet by 40 feet in size, were constructed. The fruit was turned on strip floors above a furnace. The plant had a capacity of 500 bushels a day. When the plant burned in 1900, Kimmons and Walker rebuilt and made all their construction of brick. Five kilns, 20 feet square, were enlarged in 1907 to 20 feet by 45 feet, increasing the capacity of the plant to 1,000 bushels a day.

C.B. Michelson, of the Bureau of Crop Marketing for the Frisco Railroad, wrote the following in a promotional brochure:

Returns for Their Labor

Strawberry Market on Emma Street Looking East, c. 1939. In 1907, farmers grew and harvested the greatest crop of strawberries ever known and the Arkansas strawberry remained popular far into the twentieth century. (Courtesy of Dr. J.L. Charlton and Shiloh Museum of Ozark History.)

> Springdale, Arkansas is located in the heart of the apple producing district and ships more apples annually than any other section or any one section in the entire territory served by the Frisco Railroad. Conditions in this section are ideal for the production of fruits and berries, as attested by the fact that Springdale produces a greater variety and diversity of such crops, commercially, than any other one station served by our line.

In 1920, Roscoe Steward and Professor Noyes, both of Welch's Grape Juice Company, investigated the soil around Springdale and its climate for the purpose of building a plant. For weeks, residents waited in suspense to hear the results. The establishment of such a plant would mean $400,000 in investments and employment for perhaps 200 locals. In November, J.F. Welch came from New York to announce to a meeting of more than 700 farmers, bankers, and merchants that the building of the plant in Springdale had been approved.

The company purchased several hundred acres of land and established the plant on the condition that farmers and businessmen would subscribe as much as $75,000 of stock. A minimum of 2,000 tons of grapes a year would be needed for the grape juice. This would require a minimum of 250 acres of vines. When the Welch Grape Juice Company opened their plant in 1922, the grape industry became the chief interest of the countryside. More than 1,200 acres of grapes were pledged to the factory during its first year.

A grape festival was held in Springdale on August 14, 1925. Planned as an annual celebration, and wildly successful, it was cancelled after only two seasons, perhaps because nearby Tontitown had held such a festival since 1898, or maybe there weren't enough people interested in volunteering so much time to the planning of such an event.

The 1925 festivities opened with a band concert followed by a parade that was attended by then governor Tom Terral, Senator T.H. Caraway, and Congressman J.N. Tillman. Welch Grape Juice Plant was opened to visitors. A supply of 20,000 pounds of grapes were given away free, some for eating, others in baskets for mailing. The supply was completely exhausted by 2 p.m. Nearly 4,000 baskets of grapes were mailed out of Springdale to practically every state in the country. Over 30,000 people attended the second festival in 1926. That year, 663 cars of grapes were shipped.

The Nelson Wine and Distilling Company incorporated in 1933 with a production capacity of 200,000 gallons of wine a year. The winery was built adjoining the Nelson Canning Factory.

The opening of school was delayed in 1934 by the harvest until September 10, when 851 pupils were enrolled. Tours to see the apple trees in bloom began in 1934 and attracted visitors from all over the state and nearby states as well. However, by 1937 the apple crop had been more or less displaced by grape growing and millions of pounds of grapes were annually shipped from Springdale, in addition to the large purchases by the Welch Plant. Grapes were a major crop until the Welch plant closed in the late 1970s.

The northwest Arkansas area continues to support a few large apple orchards and one is located on the eastern boundary of Springdale. Founded in 1923, Edward Gay and Sons Fruit Orchards grow apples, peaches, and grapes on 90 acres that are in danger of being usurped by the growing city. In 1930, there were

ANNUAL OZARK GRAPE FESTIVAL, 1926, LOOKING NORTH FROM HOLCOMB. The first grape festival, held in 1925, saw 20,000 pounds of grapes given away. In 1926, 30,000 people attended the festival, but it was never held in Springdale again. (Courtesy of Fay Watson and Shiloh Museum of Ozark History.)

398 farms in the township. By 1937, there were 420 with a combined acreage of 18,500. As many as 185 farms were enrolled in the soil conservation program.

The city obtained a migrant labor camp, a United States Department of Agriculture site, in 1940 for migrant farm laborers in order to provide seasonal quarters for those who flocked into the area during harvest. The camp had 200 cabins, each 14 feet square. It was abandoned by the government in 1948 and the city purchased it to continue as a service to fruit and vegetable growers. The cabins were converted from canvas roofs and sides to a permanent type with metal roofs and wooden sides. The community building on the premises was made available to the Springdale school system for classrooms and, by 1962, it was known as Jefferson School. The city agreed to continue to serve migrant workers for 20 years from the date of purchase.

It could be said that the rise of the poultry industry in northwest Arkansas was birthed by the codling moth. The apple worm (codling moth) eventually demanded all the profit from the fruit industry. Some farmers reported spraying eight to ten times per season, and the strength of the spray was continually doubled for effectiveness. Spraying was not only done more frequently, but a progressively stronger concentrate and a greater quantity of spray was necessary each time. Following several bad years where the crops froze, some farmers began to look toward a more profitable way to make a living.

As early as 1911, the University of Arkansas in Fayetteville offered courses in the care and raising of poultry. One by one, fruit farmers turned to raising chickens, passing on the word to others that it could be done, and at a profit. The first houses were small, hastily constructed structures, usually 10 to 12 feet square,

MIGRANT LABOR CAMP IN 1944. *This place was used to house migrant farm workers from 1940 through 1948. (Courtesy of Howard Clark and Shiloh Museum of Ozark History.)*

EARLY POULTRY FARM RAISING WHITE LEGHORNS. As early as 1911, the University of Arkansas offered courses in the care and raising of poultry. (Courtesy of Ray Watson and Shiloh Museum of Ozark History.)

oftentimes only a shed or a roof with chicken wire. The spaces were cleaned every week and moved around the barnyard to keep down parasites. Small wood stoves that heated the tiny houses presented a fire hazard. In those early days, chickens were allowed to range in yards during the day. Feed was not specially mixed, but rather a simple mixture of pinhead chops and homegrown corn finished with grain mix. In the beginning, chicks required 14 weeks to be ready for market, but by the 1960s, they needed only 8 or 9 weeks. The difference was due not only to better feeds, but to both improved feed and improved chicks. By this time, Arkansas stood second in the nation in poultry production.

Chickens fell prey to disease, however, since the pioneers in this new industry had very little knowledge of basic chicken diseases and husbandry. Poultry diseases continued to plague growers. In the 1920s, blood testing was begun. Coccidiosis, one of the worst poultry diseases, was a problem from the beginning, but where the disease once had to be doctored, by the 1960s, it was treated with preventive measures. Outbreaks of bronchitis were also bad at times, but the worst pullorum was eliminated through blood testing.

As early as 1921, Jeff D. Brown began raising broilers on his farm southwest of Springdale. He went to the University of Arkansas to take the examination that allowed him to be licensed as an inspector. In 1929, he became the first person to

Interior of Poultry House with Baby Chicks, c. 1935. After 1935, growers were required to conform to strict requirements for breeding, sanitation, and disease. (Courtesy of George's, Inc. and Shiloh Museum of Ozark History.)

raise chickens on a large scale when he established the Springdale Hatchery. It was the first commercial hatchery in northwest Arkansas with a 10,000-bird capacity.

It took the Great Depression to produce an environment that would lead to expansion of the poultry industry. Where other prices had plummeted, the already low chicken and egg prices did not move much. In addition, corn, the single largest component of poultry feed, was readily available and inexpensive.

In 1932, Brown put in a hatchery in Elm Springs that serviced the market in the winter and spring with a hatching of 1,500 to 1,800 chickens a week. He sold the chicks and also raised 500 chickens in two additional houses. In those days, chick sales had to be concluded by April before the summer heat. After 1935, hatcheries were required to conform to strict requirements for breeding, sanitation, and disease. Hatcheries faced other problems as well. Egg production declined in the heat, causing production costs to rise.

Despite these problems and a statement by a top administrator of the Arkansas Agricultural Experimental Station that "Poultry will never be of economic importance in Arkansas except as scavengers of waste grain and table scraps," the poultry industry soon thrived. In the spring of 1936, for example, Brown's hatchery sold more than 350,000 baby chicks and had a seasonal production of about 500,000. The eggs used were all purchased from local poultry raisers, who established their flocks from chicks purchased originally from the hatchery. Eight years after he began the hatchery, Brown had a 94,000-egg capacity hatchery in Springdale, plus a new 20,000-egg hatchery at Centerton and one that held 30,000 eggs in Fayetteville. By 1937, Brown's was the largest hatchery in the state with hatching machines having a capacity of 94,000. Long considered the father of the poultry industry, Brown once said, "The apple worm put us into the poultry business."

The main reason for the sudden growth of the poultry industry was the increased winter egg production. Poultry raisers had always believed it was not practical to attempt to secure eggs during the winter months. Limited production of fall and spring was not sufficient to justify engaging exclusively in the business. Local raisers learned that it was entirely possible and profitable to get fall and winter production from healthy and early hatched flocks. Local farmers with limited acreage did very well converting to raising poultry. Since hatcheries were locally owned, every increase in a local industry benefitted not only that industry, but the entire town and community. Poultry was an industry peculiarly suited to the climate and topography of the region.

JEFF BROWN AT FAR LEFT OF DISPLAY OF HIS POULTRY. Known as the father of the poultry industry, Brown began to raise chickens on a large scale in 1921. (Courtesy of Mrs. Jeff Brown and Shiloh Museum of Ozark History.)

Soon after opening the hatchery, Brown began his own line of feeds and mashes. He soon became known throughout the state as one of the largest dealers in poultry feeds, as well as the owner of the largest hatchery. In the early years, the feeds were tested on poultry on his farm and when proved, they were tried out on certain flocks being raised by others for him. Brown had turned the entire countryside into an experimental farm.

Besides being involved in the poultry industry on every level, Brown also served as the first president of the Arkansas Poultry Improvements Association. His hatchery employed 15 or more persons year-round, with the number greatly increased during periods of seasonal activity. White Wyandottes and White Rocks were the principal birds produced. Earl Brown, Jeff's brother, helped establish the original business, then, when a plant was opened in Fayetteville, he went there to manage it.

C.L. George and his two sons were natives of Arkansas. The family farm was located between Elm Springs and Springdale, but all three families were residents of the city for many years. In 1929, his company, C.L. George and Sons, began hauling live broilers from area growers to Kansas City and St. Louis. George's farm west of Springdale served as its first headquarters. In 1931, George opened an office on East Emma Avenue that dealt in broilers, eggs, fruits, and vegetables. The company expanded into the feed business in 1939, selling feed from other

INTERIOR OF GEORGE'S INC. BROILER HOUSE, 1942. *This picture shows coal-fired stoves, feeding, and watering equipment. (Courtesy of George's, Inc. and Shiloh Museum of Ozark History.)*

GEORGE'S, INC., FARMERS PRODUCE BUILDING AND FLEET OF TRUCKS, C. 1940. *In 1929, George and Son's began hauling live broilers from the area to Kansas City. The company expanded into the feed business in 1939. (Courtesy of George's, Inc. and Shiloh Museum of Ozark History.)*

mills. By the late 1940s, the firm was making its own feed and getting it custom-mixed. In 1959, George built a garage for his fleet of trucks and service vehicles. The following year, the live poultry building was completed. A modern hatchery was ready for use in 1961.

Hatcheries provided chicks to be grown into broilers. The next step was delivery of those broilers to the market. Farmers turned to independent truckers for the difficult transportation to markets. Some would go by train, others by truck, hauled live in cages strapped on flatbed trucks. In the winter, the cages were covered with a tarpaulin and in the spring, they were exposed.

One of the earliest pioneer truckers, J.K. Southerland, who also raised birds, told how there was no heat in the cab of the truck and he would heat a brick or rock in the fire, wrap it with burlap sacks and put it in the cab to keep from freezing. Roads weren't paved, they were muddy and deeply rutted. Truckers would drive all night to the closest city under the most dreadful of conditions. There, the truckers sold the chickens to commission agents, who, in turn, sold them to restaurants or butchers. The live birds were usually taken to Tulsa, Kansas City, Neosho, St. Louis, Springfield, and Chicago.

Birds shipped to Chicago, New York, Boston, and Philadelphia were slaughtered. Feet tied, they were packed upside-down in barrels on refrigerated train cars. They were sold as New York dressed and the cleaning was finished off

First Apple Fair. W.R. Bird is in the center foreground. The signs were made of apples. (Courtesy of Shiloh Museum of Ozark History.)

by housewives in order to save money. Live birds were also shipped by train, but they seemed to lose weight in transit and could not be shipped after the middle of May due to the heat. Truckers continued to offer the best mode of live shipment.

Other hatcheries soon followed the example of Jeff Brown. The Johnson Steele Hatchery opened for business in 1936. Joe M. Steele and Luther E. Johnson opened the Johnson and Steele Hatchery and Feeds at the corner of Graham and East Johnson Streets, with the latest in feed mixing equipment and a 20,000 capacity incubator. Johnson had a background in the poultry industry dating back to the early 1920s when he and his wife began raising hens and broilers. In 1923, they converted a piano box into a two-story chicken house, their first. They went on to raise strawberries and field tomatoes, but by 1928, they were getting serious about the chicken business. They also went into the feed business in Springdale with J.H. McKinney. From these humble beginnings, the poultry business would grow to surpass even the most optimistic entrepreneur's expectations.

Walter Bird's farm near Springdale was also in the hatchery business. Although Jeff Brown may be the father of the poultry industry, Don Tyson is today known as the king. In 1962, an article in the *Arkansas Alumnus* magazine, the official publication of the Alumni Association of the University of Arkansas, said, "[Don Tyson] . . . rules the roost of a chicken empire that produces some 25 million broilers a year, roughly one and one-half percent of all such poultry grown in the United States."

The Tyson empire began with one broken-down old truck. In the early 1930s, John Tyson, who lived in Missouri at the time, was selling produce purchased in northwest Arkansas. On one of his trips to Springdale, he noticed that some farmers were growing as many as 500 spring chickens at a time. Farmers confided in Tyson that growing them was one thing, selling them was almost impossible.

Tyson had always liked the challenge of the impossible and he took what little cash he had and bought a load of Arkansas Springs. He started out in a battered truck to sell them, although not sure where or to whom, but sell them he thought he could. He headed north, ending up in Chicago where he found a buyer and closed the deal. He made about $235 on that load. He rushed to a telegraph office and wired his original investment and his profit back home to buy more chickens. The story goes that he kept $15 to get back home, 700 miles away.

Tyson soon learned to increase load capacity by experimenting with a method of stacking and angling the makeshift coops on the flat bed. To improve the survivability of the chickens, he installed a trough to supply the birds with water and feed. Called a poultry pullman, the flatbed truck held 7,000 to 8,000 birds. The trip required 30 hours with two drivers (one was to care for the broilers). It wasn't long before Tyson moved from Missouri to Arkansas. In 1940, he started a hatchery to supply chicks to local growers and, when World War II began, the company entered the feed business. By 1950, Tyson growers were producing 500,000 birds annually.

Production doubled during the next two years and, in 1952, Tyson's son Don left the university to join the company. It seems that John called his son, who was

ONE OF THE EARLIEST PHOTOS OF THE TYSON PLANT. *In the early 1930s, Tyson began his kingdom with one broken-down old truck and enough money to make one trip from the poultry center in Arkansas to markets in Chicago. (Courtesy of Tyson's and Shiloh Museum of Ozark History.)*

JOHN TYSON (RIGHT), FOUNDER OF TYSON'S FOODS, WITH HIS SON DON. By 1962, John Tyson ruled the roost of the chicken empire and was known as the king. His son Don would soon take over the title. (Courtesy of Tyson's and Shiloh Museum of Ozark History.)

in his senior year at the university, and said that he had a chance to sell the company. Don is reported to have replied, "For gosh sakes, don't sell! I'll be there in 15 minutes." In reality, he finished the semester first. At the age of 22, he assumed the responsibilities of general manager. In February 1968, John Tyson and his wife, Helen, were killed in a collision with a train at the Highway 264 railroad crossing.

Though it has had its ups and downs, the poultry industry continued to flourish through the 1960s. Asked what he thought of the future of the industry in 1962, Don Tyson replied, "At times, it's been like sitting in the front seat of a roller coaster. But what a ride!"

It didn't take long for the poultry industry to father a second industry in the lush farmland countryside. Farmers realized that the availability of chicken litter to fertilize pastures would make ideal grazing land for cattle. The experimental station at the University of Arkansas soon became quite active in livestock research in addition to that of poultry. The combination of beef cattle and poultry put Washington and Benton Counties on top agriculturally in the state. Today, in the green valleys of fescue grass throughout northwest Arkansas, large herds of top-quality cattle graze contentedly alongside gleaming metal poultry houses.

POULTRY JUDGING. *White Rocks and White Wyandottes were the principal birds being bred. By 1962, Arkansas growers were raising 25 million broilers each year. (Courtesy of Carroll County Heritage Center and Shiloh Museum of Ozark History.)*

7. Law and Order, or Else

When the shooting started out in the street and bodies began falling, the search was on for [Constable] Shankles. Someone found him in the Concord Theater lobby. When told there was a big shooting up the street and two or three were dead already, he asked, "Do they have guns?"

"Of course they have guns," the citizen told the reluctant officer. He then wanted to know if they were still shooting. The citizen, growing rather exasperated, replied that yes, they were still shooting.

"Well," said Lee. "Let's just wait a few more minutes. Then we'll go have a look."

—Excerpt from *Emma We Love You* by Bruce Vaughan

The city's first jail was erected soon after incorporation in 1878. Eight feet square, it was constructed of 2-inch-by-6-inch oak lumber laid flat like logs. The floor, of the same heavy material, was laid the same way. There was one massive door with a huge lock and iron bars across the outside. The little window, measuring 6 inches by 8 inches, also had bars across it. The town marshal, who served as custodian of the jail, was paid in part by a percentage of the fines levied against the inmates. Cases were tried before the mayor, who also assessed those fines for a variety of violations: playing marbles, throwing horseshoes on the main street, throwing a ball or running a horse in town, gambling and horse racing, operating bawdy houses. Laws passed by the council in 1888 were meant to protect public morals.

It is said that once, when the city branch that ran through Springdale went on an unusually wild spree, the little jail went floating off. Luckily, there were no prisoners at the time. It must have been either rebuilt or captured and replaced, because jail facilities were not moved to city hall until much later. Though the jail was constructed in 1878 and no doubt some citizens were incarcerated there, the first town ordinance was not actually passed until 1880. It forbade "noises, fighting, guns, firecrackers and rock throwing in the city limits." Fines were also levied on those who disturbed religious services or drove faster than a trot.

A preacher and school teacher charged with giving one of his 13-year-old pupils 45 licks was tried in justice court in 1887. Because of the crowd, the trial was moved to the Baptist Church. Millard Berry was attorney for the state and White Walker for the defense. The verdict was "not guilty."

LOOKING WEST ON EMMA AVENUE, BETWEEN 1913 AND 1925. By 1911, traffic had become such a problem on Emma and other city streets that the city decided to begin to enforce the state automobile laws of a 15-mile-per-hour speed limit.

Although uncontrolled making and selling of liquor was technically legal until Prohibition went into nationwide effect on January 17, 1919, there was a clean-up of blind tigers on February 27, 1891. It isn't clear who led the clean-up, but it might have been Shelby Todhunter, a pioneer peace officer. It is recorded that he apprehended robbers within 18 hours after a big robbery in Springdale in 1895, so he could have been serving as early as 1891.

In the county, it was common for farmers to earn a little extra on the side by distilling their own brand of home brew. Stills could be found alongside streams in many areas, especially farther south in the rugged hill country. Also common in these rural areas was a barrel of moonshine beside the road with a cup hanging nearby so travelers could taste the offering.

On August 14, 1905, an editorial in the *Springdale News* proclaimed the following:

> As an example of freak legislation the curfew ordinance passed by the town council probably equals anything that was ever ground out by any law making body. It surpasses that wildest dream of the average Arkansas legislator, and its parallel will doubtless not be found this side of Kansas.
>
> The Ordinance, in effect, says that no person under 20 years of age, be he Jew or gentile, saint or sinner, male or female, white or black, is to

be allowed on the streets or alleys or vacant lots of the incorporated town of Springdale at any hour of the night, for any purpose, even by and with the consent of their parents, guardians, protectors, defenders and keepers.

It makes no difference whether they be going for the doctor, preacher, lawyer or undertaker. The *News* very much doubts the good that would result from a curfew law of any kind, believing that a good rawhide properly administered by the pater familias would reach the spot quicker.

We now have the law. Let it be enforced. Let the marshal and his deputies station themselves on the street corner next Sunday night after church services and arrest every young man and young woman under 20 years of age who are not under the protecting wing of their parents and confine them in the calaboose until 9 o'clock Monday morning.

On May 10, 1907, the city council passed an ordinance against cattle running freely on the city streets. And in 1911, traffic became such a problem that the mayor warned that the state automobile laws would be enforced: "a 15-mph speed limit, and a requirement that motorists approaching a horse must stop and remain stopped until the horse had passed."

The Bank of Springdale was robbed only twice in 50 years, but both were the talk of the town. On December 19, 1901, shortly before noon, a lone masked

City Directors, 1904. From left to right are (front row) C.L. Thompson, recorder; and I.T. Lane, mayor; (back row) C.G. Dodson, W.H. Searcy, B.F. Young, J.M. Howitt, J.H. Myers, W.A. Graves, and Newt Henson, nightwatch. (Courtesy of Mrs. L.W. Searcy and Shiloh Museum of Ozark History.)

robber scooped up all the ready cash, took an armful of packages of new currency from the vault and fled into the hills with officers and citizens in hot pursuit.

W.A. Graves, assistant cashier, was alone in the bank when the robber entered, cashier J.P. Deaver having stepped out a few minutes before. J.S. Dodson entered the bank while the robbery was in progress and was the direct cause of the robber's precipitate flight. The thief ran to his horse and buggy, which he had hitched in the rear of Pollock's Furniture store, and galloped out of town, but turned his horse loose a mile from town and took to the hills on foot. He was described as a small man, about 25 years old. Bloodhounds from a convict camp at Prairie Grove arrived in the afternoon and were put on the trail. The total amount of money taken from the bank was $5,515, but the robber lost $1,485 in his flight. A search of the hills revealed the remainder of the money and all but $655 was recovered. The robber was caught in Fayetteville and sentenced to three years.

The second robbery took place in October of 1931, after the bank merged with the First National Bank. Four unmasked men walked into the bank and relieved tellers of $5,000. They escaped into the Cookson Hills of Oklahoma with lawmen in hot pursuit. Although an arrest was made, nobody was ever convicted of this robbery.

April 1915 was a particularly exciting month in the lives of local residents. A bloody fight broke out at the corner of Holcomb Street and Emma Avenue on a Sunday afternoon, there was an attempted jail break, and a threat was made by the city council to resign unless Mayor I.T. Lane resigned.

Automobile thieves raided the town in January of 1923 and stole two cars. That year, 148 auto owners paid their city license. On November 20, 1925, a woman was arrested for mailing dynamite at the Springdale post office. On January 16, 1932, two robbers held up Coger Drug. On May 1, 1934, two men robbed the Western Union Office.

Until 1913 citizens all voted as one, then four wards were established and the city voted by wards for the first time in the city election. W.G. Ownbey was re-elected mayor in that year. After prohibition was repealed in 1933, it would be another ten years before the city addressed the issue of liquor sales directly with the voters. When they did, wards one and four voted "wet" on February 9, 1943, and the city voted "wet" on March 23, 1943, but no vote was held in wards two and three. As the state law reads, if no vote is held, then it is automatically "wet."

The Alcohol Beverage Control, a regulatory agency in the state, had a tough time with enforcement because the wet/dry issue was so confusing within each county, township, city, and ward. In the state of Arkansas, liquor by the bottle cannot be sold anywhere but a liquor store and only in wards, cities, townships, or counties where it has been so voted, or not, as the case may be. That ordinance includes beer and wine. In 1999, a law was passed that allows liquor by the drink to be sold in restaurants so licensed. Only recently, a new law went into effect that allows grocery stores to sell Arkansas wines.

Though no reports of a great increase in crime were recorded, enforcing the law must have grown a bit more difficult. Or maybe the town simply felt growing pains. In 1935, in addition to the regular constable, Len Henson was hired to fill a new position, that of city jailer.

Over the years, various speed limits had been set for city streets. Back in the days of the horse and buggy and bicycles, 15 miles per hour was fine, but by 1907, after Emma was graveled for the first time and bridges built, it was raised to 25 miles per hour. By 1911, there were 25 cars moving about the streets, but it wasn't until 1937 that the speed limit was fixed and strictly enforced at 25 miles per hour.

In 1943, a triple murder occurred that was to be the last killing in the city until 1972. This story was told to Bruce Vaughan by Rueben Bryant, and published in Vaughan's book, *Emma We Love You*. The city had no police department at the time of the triple murder. Lee Shankles was its peace officer or constable. When the shooting started out in the street and bodies began falling, the search was on for Shankles. Someone found him in the Concord Theater lobby. When told there was a big shooting up the street and two or three were dead already, he asked, "Do they have guns?"

Of course they had guns, the citizen told the reluctant officer. He wanted to know if they were still shooting. The citizen, growing rather exasperated, replied that yes, they were still shooting. "Well," said Lee. "Let's just wait a few more minutes. Then we'll go have a look."

Tuck Bishop, the shooter, was arrested in Alma approximately 22 hours later. He and the girl he was with were taken off the bus in Alma. He was convicted and went to the Arkansas State Penitentiary, but in 1945, Bishop was granted a Christmas furlough. He took off for the state of Utah where he committed two more murders. He allegedly stayed in prison in Utah until, near death, he was released to go back to his home in Berryville where he died in 1977.

Up to the time of the Bishop murders, peace officers had little to do. Duties were confined to arresting disorderly drunks and it seems that Lee Shankles had a way about him when it came to calming out-of-control drunks. Bruce Vaughan wrote the following in *Emma We Love You*:

> He carried a night stick that was rumored to be filled with lead. He first placed the offender under arrest; then if the celebrant offered enough resistance, Lee swung his stick, hitting the offender in the side of the head. This seemed to have a soothing effect on the more violent types. On rare occasions a second blow might be required.

It was probably the Bishop murders that convinced the citizenry that the town needed a real chief of police and so, in 1946, S.R. "Cy" Phillips took on the duties, which continued to consist of arresting drunks, checking doors at night, and writing parking tickets.

The appointment of Wayne Hyden as chief of police in 1952 marked the beginning of a modern police force for the city. Hyden was formerly a trooper with the Arkansas State Police stationed in Fayetteville. According to city prosecutor Jeff Harper, Hyden took the Springdale Police Department from the

SPRINGDALE POLICE DEPARTMENT, 1958, DURING FIVE-DAY TRAINING SESSION. *From left to right are the following: (front row) Frank Sims, Speedy Wilson, Wayne Hyden, Pete Peterson, and unidentified; (back row) Joe Sims, Morgan Carson, Ed Terry, Bill Smith, Guy Smith, Stanley Black, Herman McCullough, and Eldon Martens. Wayne Hyden was the city's first chief of police, appointed in 1952. (Courtesy of Ollen Stepp, Mrs. Wayne Hyden, and Shiloh Museum of Ozark History.)*

level of law enforcement previously described to a modern day law enforcement agency. From the time Hyden took over until the early 1970s, Springdale did not have any high profile major crimes of note. Hyden retired in 1973, then became Director of Community Development and served in this position until 1992. He died on January 18, 1995.

When Hyden started in 1952, he had three officers. The first uniform they wore consisted of a brown shirt, light brown pants with a dark brown stripe, and a dark green coat. In the 1960s, Hyden changed the uniform to gray and it is still in use today. An "Ike" jacket was worn by officers during cold weather, but they did not have an issued heavy coat.

Joe Sims, who became a police officer in the city under Hyden in the 1950s and retired as chief of police of Springdale in 1976, described Hyden's department as follows: "Under Hyden, the Springdale Police Department became a modern day police department. Hyden believed in strict, tough enforcement of the law, but in being fair while doing it."

After the farmers' and laborers' movements for social change swept Washington County in the 1870s, 1880s, and 1890s, the People's Progressive Party (PPP), with

FORMER CHURCH USED AS CITY HALL FROM 1930 THROUGH 1960. Built in 1910 by former First Baptist Church members, it later housed Central Presbyterian Church. (Courtesy of Springdale News *and Shiloh Museum of Ozark History.)*

its similar politics, took over the political scene. Early in the twentieth century, socialism had some followers in Springdale in the guise of several organizations dedicated to the interests of workers. Stanley J. Clark, national organizer for the Socialist Party, debated J.H. Amacher of Springdale on the merits of socialism in 1909. By 1924, the PPP had grown to some prominence throughout the county. The organization opposed the financial tyranny of big financial monopolies and demanded government operated banks that would loan money at low interest rates to ordinary citizens. It also called for "equal rights for women in every walk of life, and legislation protecting the child life of this Nation."

During the early growth years, city hall was located in a converted Central Presbyterian Church. In 1959, a new city hall was constructed and the jail moved to this location in 1960. The city is ruled by a mayor-council city government. The mayor serves a term of four years and aldermen serve one-year terms. Mayors of Springdale include the following names:

Joe Holcomb, 1879–1881
R.M. Huffmaster, 1881–1882
O.C. Ludwig, 1882–1883
Joe Holcomb, 1883–1884
William G. Pruner, 1884–1885
S.L. Staples, 1885–1887

Millard Berry, 1887–1890
C.J. Chapman, 1890–1894
S.N. Haxton, 1894–1897
E.H. Bryant, 1897–1898
C.J. Chapman, 1898–1901
L.D. Petross, 1901–1902
J.J. Long, 1902–1904
I.T. Lane, 1904–1907
William Focht, 1907–1908
John A. Joyce, 1909–1910
J.M. Hewitt, 1910–1911
E.S. Thompson, 1911–1912
W.G. Ownbey, 1912–1914
I.T. Lane, 1914–1916
L.A. Smith, 1916–1918
Charles Smyer, 1918–1919
J.S. Ewalt, 1919–1921
H.B. Rice, 1921–1922

RICHARD M. HUFFMASTER AND WIFE. *He served as the second mayor from 1881 to 1882. (Courtesy of Ethel Wright and Shiloh Museum of Ozark History.)*

J.S. Ewalt, 1922–1924
W.A. Graves, 1924–1926
G.T. Sullins, 1926–1928
Paul Butler, 1928–1930
F.F. Hazel, 1930–1932
F.D. Watson, 1932–1936
Courtney Crouch, 1936–1938
W.G. Howard, 1938–1944
H.D. Ewalt, 1944–1947
Elmer Johnson, 1947–1952
H.R. Sharp, 1952–1954
Hugh O. Sherry, 1954–1960
John W. Powell, 1960–1962
Charles Davis, 1962–1966
Park Phillips, 1967–1974
Roy C. Ritter, 1975–1978
Charles N. McKinney, 1978–2000
Jerre Van Hoose, 2000–Present

JOSEPH S. EWALT. *He served as mayor from 1919 to 1921 and from 1922 to 1924. (Courtesy of Shiloh Museum of Ozark History.)*

8. That's Entertainment

The band furnished good music. Jim Wilson played the Dutchman nicely. Miss Annie Walden's piece was good. Ed Hale's "Yaller Gal" was immense. Enough to make a sick mule smile. Hugh Phillips trod the boards like an old veteran. Miss Fannie Givens' piece was spoken very natural. Miss Cener Holcomb did extremely well. And the supper—well, we're too full for utterance.
—Springdale News *on the Entertainment and Strawberry Festival, 1894*

Before the turn of the twentieth century, entertainment usually meant a great deal of people getting together to celebrate something, anything. Picnics were extremely popular, as were hay rides, spelling bees, pie suppers, musicals, and literaries. For a short time, baby shows, akin to today's beauty pageants, attracted some attention, but their popularity soon waned. A rousing parade often kicked off these events, the most popular of which was the Fourth of July celebration and picnic. In 1887, there were also speeches, band music, races, and a ball game between Springdale and Bentonville, followed by a fireworks display.

In their daily lives, people labored long and hard, but the old adage, "all work and no play . . ." was taken seriously. There were taffy pulls at the Grand Army of the Republic (GAR) Hall, moonlight picnics, and an occasional masquerade or lecture to attend. When a medicine show appeared in one of the upstairs halls in September of 1887, the editor of the *News* wrote, "The circus was a good little show." The Springdale Literary and Dramatic Society often presented entertainment to celebrate Christmas at the school house with fireworks afterwards.

Crokinole parties were all the rage. Crokinole is a board game in which flat pieces much like those used in Tiddly Winks are flipped to score. The name is taken from the French Croquignole, a small hard biscuit that the disks resemble. The oldest known American board has inscribed on its bottom "Crokinole, M.B. Ross, New York, Pat. Apr. 20, 1880."

In 1892, the popular Dramatic Club presented as its initial performance *Broken Fetters*. That year, Gebbert and Hunt installed a stage with a drop curtain in their hall for such presentations and, in 1894, the Opera House was built, complete with stage, drop curtain, folding seats, and everything except scenery. Traveling companies furnished their own.

That's Entertainment

Fourth of July Parade on Emma Avenue, c. 1901. The view is looking east from Holcomb and Emma. (Courtesy of Marion S. Warner, Estate of W.G. Howard, and Shiloh Museum of Ozark History.)

That same year, the entertainment and strawberry festival at the school house was a decided success. Coverage in the *News* reported the following:

> The band furnished good music. Jim Wilson played the Dutchman nicely. Miss Annie Walden's piece was good. Ed Hale's "Yaller Gal" was immense. Enough to make a sick mule smile. Hugh Phillips trod the boards like an old veteran. Miss Fannie Givens' piece was spoken very natural. Miss Cener Holcomb did extremely well. And the supper—well, we're too full for utterance.

The Springdale Baseball Association was organized on May 13, 1891, with 17 members. The team lost its first two games to Fayetteville and Rogers. The next year, Springdale defeated Fayetteviile at the Fourth of July celebration. The popular airplane, the Curtiss JN.4D, affectionately known as the Flying Jenny, was the chief amusement attraction at the picnic that year, according to the 1937 issue of the *News*. Since the Flying Jenny was in production from 1909 through 1919, and barnstormers were all the vogue, the Jenny probably did fly during a Fourth of July Picnic celebration, but not in the late 1890s.

By 1903, the popularity of baseball saw the team play 19 games, winning 13 and losing 6. For the Fourth of July celebration in 1910, a musical and literary program was given in the morning. There were races and a band concert in the afternoon and a balloon ascension and parachute leap in the evening. For some reason, a fireworks display was banned that year, but that prohibition did not last.

In 1922, baseball fans met at the Springdale Drug Company and organized a team to be known as the Springdale Orphans because they had no home grounds. The school refused to allow the ball team to use the school field. On June 9, there was a big celebration at the opening of the new ball park. Unfortunately, the bleachers collapsed, and the fire company immediately responded to an alarm. But since no one was badly injured and a good time was had by all, the opening of the new ball park was considered a grand success. Mayor Ewalt made a speech, the band played, and the baseball team lost to Rogers 3 to 9.

The Opera House opened on September 21, 1894, with a performance of *Louva the Pauper* by local young society people. With the building of the Opera House, show troupes came. The Blind Boone Concert Company played; the Crow Dramatic Company performed in *Count of Monte Cristo*; the Frank Griswold Company presented *Uncle Tom's Cabin*. For a number of years, Belcer's Comedians made an annual appearance.

Chautauquas flowered in the gay 1890s and first came to Springdale in 1898. During that time, Josiah H. Shinn, author, historian, and educator, was president of Springdale College and had a considerable influence on the cultural life of the town. He first introduced the chautauqua there and in other towns in Arkansas. The first one was held in a tent from July 4 through July 17, 1898. It was an artistic success, though a financial failure.

Lectures were a preferred entertainment at the chautauquas in the early years and included such notable platform figures as William Jennings Bryan, who

WILLIAM JENNINGS BRYAN'S ARRIVAL BY TRAIN ON JULY 24, 1899. *He came to lecture at chautauqua. (Courtesy of Washington County Historical Society and Shiloh Museum of Ozark History.)*

served as secretary of state under President Woodrow Wilson and ran unsuccessfully three times for the office of President of the United States. Special trains were run on the day the popular Bryan spoke and the attendance was estimated at 10,000. Over the years, other notable speakers were Champ Clark; the noted poet Edmund Vance Cooke; General John B. Gordon of Georgia; Colonel George W. Bain; Senator John Ingalls of Kansas; the noted editor John Temple Graves of Atlanta; Colonel H.W.J. Ham; and two Arkansas favorites, Governor Dan W. Jones and ex-governor William M. Fishback. Music was furnished by the Springdale band and the Wagner Male Concert Company. Professor William Apmadoc was in charge of singing during the entire week. July 16 was declared Arkansas Day with an address by President John L. Buchanan of the University of Fayetteville.

By 1902, Josiah H. Shinn had left Springdale and a chautauqua association was organized with E.C. Pritchard as chairman and John P. Stafford as secretary. An auditorium was built in the fall of 1904 where chautauquas and other community gatherings were held. Later, it was used by the high school as a gymnasium.

On September 29, 1905, silver trophies were awarded to Claire Jessamine Brandon and Maud Pardue, winners of the baby show. That same year, over 500 season tickets were sold to the eighth chautauqua held from July 16 through July

CARRIE NATION ENJOYING A DRINK OF EUREKA SPRINGS WATER. *She later appeared at a Chautauqua in Springdale. (Courtesy of Carroll County Heritage Center and Shiloh Museum of Ozark History.)*

23. Carrie Nation, the famed prohibitionist, who was 60 years old at the time, visited and spoke at the auditorium. The *News* reported that her talk was rambling, but she attracted much attention on the street. The 1906 chautauqua introduced moving pictures to astounded audiences. The American Vitagraph Company gave a 40-minute showing, but it would be a couple of years before this form of entertainment caught on.

Minstrel shows attracted good crowds, as did Shakespeare productions. In 1908, 16 footlights and 15 upper lights were installed on the stage. One of the most elaborate programs ever given was produced that year when Dr. A.C. Smith was manager. It included moving pictures by the Hite-Monroe Moving Picture Company, Reno and Hunneston, magicians, the Kellogg-Haynes Concert Company, song recitals, and Pitt Parker, a cartoonist. Frederick Warde appeared in some of the Shakespeare productions. Among many others on the program were the balloon ascension and parachute jump. Four thousand people attended on July 4 alone. For the seasons of 1909 and 1910, however, attendance and interest had lagged, and the chautauqua was discontinued for several years. Other, more modern entertainments waited in the wings, poised to replace the chautauqua.

In March 1910, Charles Renner and John Stafford leased the Long Building on Emma Avenue to give the town an up-to-date motion picture theater. Live stage presentations remained popular and the theatrical season continued.

For a brief time, the chautauqua was revived in 1916 when the Springdale Chautauqua Association was organized with John. C. Anderson as president. In July 1919, a three-day chautauqua was held. In that same year, a three-day indoor chautauqua was staged in the auditorium, but despite all efforts, attendance was poor and the event suffered a financial loss.

When Rudolph Valentino appeared in the moving picture *The Sheik* on March 31, 1922, the entire family was admitted to the theater for 25¢. The first talkies presented in 1929 at the Concord Theater proved unsatisfactory, and when the Concord reopened in July, it went back to silent pictures. Then, on January 6, 1930, the theater put in a new sound system and talkies had arrived to stay. The motion picture *Street Girl* was the first to be shown with the new system.

The chautauqua auditorium was sold and torn down in 1932. Other forms of entertainment had dealt a severe blow to the so-long-popular chautauqua. In 1998 and 1999, Shiloh Museum brought back the popular entertainment, with reenactments of the appearance of William Jennings Bryan and Carrie Nation.

About the same time as moving pictures were in their infancy, the magic of radio caught on, mesmerizing those hungry for entertainment. For Christmas in 1921, Robert H. Clark received a one-vacuum tube receiver made by the maker of American Flyer toy trains. It was the first vacuum tube receiver in town. One night, he heard music and voices from station KDKA in Pittsburgh, Pennsylvania. The broadcast could only be listened to by one person at a time using earphones. His father was so impressed with this new gadget that he decided he and his son could build something so a roomful of people could hear. It took three months to secure parts and complete construction of a breadboard model, then his father had a beautiful solid walnut cabinet made for it. For many months, the model remained in the attic near the wire antenna, but there were more visitors to that attic than it could hold. The family obtained a Magnavox horn-type loud speaker and sometimes, there would be up to 50 people in the backyard listening to the broadcasts.

Near the end of the war, in 1944, a group of men seriously settled down to staging a rodeo. Thurman "Shorty" Parsons, Dempsey Letch, and Walter Watkins Sr. were instrumental in planning the event. Parsons's life included a long list of civic duties and accomplishments. He reasoned that with the war going on and rationing of tires and gasoline, people couldn't travel easily. They needed something they could enjoy close to home. Members of the Clarence E. Beeley Post of the American Legion and the chamber of commerce stepped forward and rented the area behind the sale barn for $50, portable seats were arranged, and the first rodeo was set to open over the July Fourth holiday.

A collapse of the north side bleachers sent 300 people to the hospital, but none were seriously injured. In spite of this setback, the first rodeo proved so successful that soon after the final performance, another was scheduled for the following year. It, too, was a success. July Fourth became the event's permanent date, the ideal time for a parade, a picnic, and a rodeo followed by fireworks. Crowds grew larger every year and, eventually, the Springdale Benevolent Amusement Association was formed in order to better promote and stage the event. Stock sold to businessmen throughout the entire area. Wooden stands seated 2,500 in the first stadium, named after Shorty Parsons. By 1962, an all-steel bowl comfortably seated 12,000 and the 4-day event attracted nearly 30,000 people.

Besides being the top tourist attraction, the Springdale rodeo is one of the largest professional rodeos of the southwest. It is rated among the top rodeo attractions of the nation during the July Fourth holidays. All competitors are members of the Professional Rodeo Cowboys Association (PRCA) and compete for big prize money every year. As many as nine world champions or former champions have competed in a single show at the arena.

In March 1975, the Rodeo Community Building on Old Missouri Road was dedicated. The building, which seats 1,500, was constructed for use by civic, cultural, and commercial groups in northwest Arkansas. The south side of the outdoor rodeo arena was equipped with aluminum bleachers and covered in 1995, and, by 1997, work had begun to renovate the west side, which was finished in 2000. The remainder of the arena roof will be finished as funds become available. After serving as president of the Rodeo of the Ozarks for 38 years, Shorty Parsons passed away in 1988.

Today, the PRCA rodeo and connected events, such as street dances, window decorations by merchants, BBQs, and two parades attract crowds upwards of 50,000 people. John Reddish is currently president of the Benevolent Amusement Association, which sponsors the rodeo and a host of other events in the area.

The arts hold a special place in the hearts and minds of Springdale's residents, and to fill that need, the Springdale Fine Arts Center was organized in 1967. In

KENNETH ADAMS THROWN FROM A BULL IN SPRINGDALE PRCA RODEO. *The Springdale rodeo is one of the professional rodeos of the southwest and is a principal tourist attraction. (Courtesy of Springdale Chamber of Commerce and Shiloh Museum of Ozark History.)*

1972, the Art Center of the Ozarks (ACO) was founded. The center acquired a permanent home when it purchased the First Christian Church building on Grove Avenue. The sanctuary was converted into the Wagon Wheel Theater and the rest of the building is used for art projects and a theater support system.

The ACO is a privately incorporated, non-profit educational arts institution governed by a 40-member board of directors. The art center owns the old Bobby Hopper Ford dealership adjacent to it. All they need now is about $5 million to turn it into the performing and classroom space the ACO's patrons want. The community has always been instrumental in the expansions and the center would like to come into this one with some major grant money. The current facility, opened in April 1993, includes the Bernice Jones Theater, which seats 425; the Smith Kelly Performance Hall and Gallery, a 125-seat flexible performing and gallery space; the McCuistion-Matthews Gallery and lobby area; the Walker Administrative Office Wing; the Tyson Education Wing with visual arts classrooms and dance studio; a 20-seat conference room; a theater scene shop; a

ARTS CENTER OF THE OZARKS. *This privately incorporated, non-profit educational arts institution is governed by a 40-member board of directors. (Courtesy of Arts Center of the Ozarks.)*

costume shop; dressing rooms; a greenroom; a catering kitchen; and storage areas. The center offers cutting-edge drama, slapstick comedy, classic mysteries, and even an occasional shocker. The big theater is booked about 300 nights a year.

It is clear that the rich history of Springdale deserves professional preservation for all generations to come. The Shiloh Museum was founded for just that purpose. Mary Parsons wrote in *Washington County History*, published by the Shiloh Museum in 1989, that "The Shiloh Museum, established by the City of Springdale, has as its purpose the preservation of the heritage of Northwest Arkansas through the collection, exhibition and interpretation of objects which illustrate the story of man in this area."

The museum committee, appointed by Mayor Park Phillips, included Charles McKinney as chairman and Espen Walters, E.A. Chandler, and Joe Robinson as members. The bylaws were approved in May of 1968. The museum opened to the public on September 7, 1968, at Johnson and Main Streets in the historic district of Springdale in the building that originally housed the public library. On opening day, the featured exhibit was a significant collection of Native American artifacts from Judge Guy W. Howard.

Howard came to town in 1892 and served as city attorney for 12 years. He read law under the late I.M. Davis and was admitted to the bar in 1907. Howard went on to practice until his death in the 1960s. He became an important civic leader and an avid collector of prehistoric and historic Native American artifacts of this area. He was a great collector of curiosities and turned his home into a museum. His collection became the basis for Shiloh Museum's earliest exhibits. Purchased by the museum in 1965, it contains over 10,000 artifacts and 260 books, pamphlets, bulletins, and more on archaeology and anthropology. Besides the Howard Collection of Indian Artifacts, collections include the Vaughn-Applegate Collection of antique photographic equipment, the Jeanne Hoffer-Tucker Collection of Essie Ward paintings, the Mooney-Barker Drugstore Collection, and a historic photograph collection of more than 40,000 images.

The first board of directors at Shiloh Museum included Charles Davis, chairman; Leon Allen, vice-president; John Cagle, secretary; Annabel Searcy, treasurer; and D. Dupree Deaver, Betty Hornor, Charles McKinney, Joe Robinson, and Larry Swaim, board members. Directors of the museum have been Linda Allen Hild, from 1968 to 1975 and 1976 to 1980; Marlene Hartzler in 1975; Betty Hornor in 1976; and currently, Bob Besom, who has served since 1980.

Volunteers have played an important role in the development of the museum. The Friends of the Shiloh Museum volunteer association was formed in 1985 to support the activities of the museum. In 1988, 47 volunteers worked over 1,500 hours. Over the years, through several revisions of the bylaws, the board of trustees has expanded the field of interest to include all six counties of northwest Arkansas: Benton, Boone, Carroll, Newton, Madison, and Washington.

By 1989, over $500,000 was raised to erect an 18,000-square-foot complex, which includes exhibit galleries, auditorium, library and archives, offices, and storage areas. The city of Springdale supported the project with additional funds and remains its main source of financial support, though approximately two-thirds of its members, visitors, and participants live outside Springdale.

THE FIRST HOME OF THE SHILOH MUSEUM IN THE OLD PUBLIC LIBRARY BUILDING, 1969. *On opening day in September 1968, the featured exhibit was a collection of artifacts belonging to Judge Guy W. Howard. (Courtesy of Shiloh Museum of Ozark History.)*

In 1991, the museum held its grand opening of the new facilities. Several renovated historic structures have been moved to the museum grounds: the Cooper Barn, the Steele General Store, Dr. John C. Carter's Office, the Cartmell Outhouse, and the Ritter-McDonald Log Cabin. The Searcy House was already on the site.

An enormously popular form of entertainment appeared the same year that the Shiloh Museum opened its doors. In 1968, the Albert E. Brumley Memorial Sundown to Sunup Singing Festival entertained a large, enthusiastic audience. During its first year in Springdale, the festival to honor the accomplishments of Albert Brumley, who wrote about 200 gospel songs, took in $100. Originally, chamber officials were reluctant to hold the festival here, feeling the venture would be more trouble than it was worth. However, by 1983, the festival was one of the chamber's major events, attracting some of the biggest performers in the gospel industry. At least 75 ticket sellers are involved and there is a massive advertising campaign in five surrounding states.

Though billed as a dusk to dawn performance, in actuality the festival begins at 7 p.m. and the latest it has continued is 3 a.m. It has always been held in the rodeo arena but recently moved to the Randall Tyson Arena in Fayetteville. Today, the sundown to sunup sing is a cornerstone of the tourist industry in the area.

WENDY BAGWELL AND THE SUNLITERS, 1984. *The group appears at the annual Albert Brumley All Night Gospel Sing. (Courtesy of Springdale Chamber of Commerce and Shiloh Museum of Ozark History.)*

9. Guns of War

. . . A wife, children, father and mother, and sister and perhaps a brother at home in Arkansas not knowing that I am alive. Two years have almost passed since I saw them, and war is yet moving onward, recruiting for death, marching her thousands to the grave. How long will times thus go on? When shall the Angel of Death stay his arm of revenge and wing his flight to other realms, and Mercy, the Angel of Peace, shall revisit us with the olive branch entwined around her radiant brow, saying "Peace, be still." Then shall the weary soldier return to his friends and home of former days.

—From the diary of Evans Atwood, Civil War soldier

A scattering of men in the county answered a call to arms in 1847 and fought with Archibald Yell's company of volunteers in the War with Mexico, the first conflict they would take part in as settlers in this new land.

Because the Civil War was fought on the very soil on which the Shiloh pioneers had settled, it would be devastating to those families who lived here. Later wars, with their battles in places like the Marne and Tripoli, Iwo Jima and Midway, the conflicts in Korea and Vietnam, the Gulf and Afghanistan, all would take their toll, in both military and civilian deaths, but this civil conflict destroyed homes and businesses in our own hometowns and ripped apart the fabric of our nation. In the South, in Arkansas, in Shiloh, it would take decades to heal the scars.

The issue of slavery intertwined with states rights and to those living in Arkansas, it became a matter of whether or not the national government had the right to compel states to follow federal law. This has long been an argument that cannot be settled here. Few of those living in Shiloh owned slaves, most despised the idea of slavery, yet, in many cases, they would side with the South in its struggle to place the rights of states above the rights of the federal government to rule those states. At the same time, many saw secession as traitorous and destructive to the country that they loved.

With residents of the area divided in their sympathies, regiments for both the Union and the Confederacy formed up, ripping families apart and creating a dangerous climate for soldier and civilian alike. Following major battles at Pea Ridge and Prairie Grove, the region was left to bushwhackers, who roamed the countryside, burning, looting, and ravaging. Women and children, defenseless in the absence of husbands, brothers, fathers, and uncles, were at the mercy of these hooligans, who swore no allegiance save that of greed and brutality.

Families who settled in and around Shiloh all had relatives who had fought under the American flag in their country's wars: the Revolution of 1776, the War of 1812, the Seminole War in 1835, and the Mexican War in 1847. Staunch patriotism to their country and its flag was not new to these pioneers. Even as the rumblings of war were heard across the land, residents were of a divided mind. When Washington County voters were invited to the polls, they rejected a state convention that would consider secession and gave huge majorities to delegates pledged to moderation, which meant the majority supported remaining in the Union.

The decision to stand with the Union continued even as war broke out and President Lincoln called upon Arkansas to muster to arms. To the surprise and disappointment of many, the convention of May 6 took Arkansas out of the Union. Under continued pressure from secessionists, each delegate reluctantly changed his vote until it was left to Isaac Murphy, who staunchly declined, saying he would gladly lay down his life for the benefit of the Southern states. He warned of the untold evils that would follow secession and voted a resounding "NO." Nevertheless, the measure passed, and Arkansas seceded from the Union. Murphy was elected governor of Arkansas once that horrendous war was over and the Union had prevailed.

Debates tore families apart before the war could do so. Remembered as a war that cast brother against brother, this could not have been more true than it was in the border states of Arkansas, which seceded, and Missouri, which remained in the Union. Citizens of both states were almost equally divided in their sympathies. Ultimately, the victims of such divided loyalties were the women, their children, and the elderly, who remained at home to live literally "on the battlefield." No matter on which side a man's loyalties lay, he and his family would become involved in the battles, would suffer greatly and die for their beliefs, some bloodying the very soil they had once tilled.

Shiloh was badly damaged during the Civil War, and most of its homes and businesses were burned, as well as the beloved Shiloh Church. On September 6, a Sunday in 1863, heavy fighting took place between the Fitzgerald and Holcombe homes on Wire Road. This is believed to be the night that the Shiloh Baptist Church was burned, along with several other homes in Shiloh. Silas Graham and his family were left homeless when their house was burned during the Civil War and, like so many others, he fled to Texas with his mother and brother in a cart drawn by a yoked bull and heifer. The family returned to Arkansas after the war. He married Lucinda Wilson in 1886 and they had two children. He served the town as a blacksmith for 40 years.

Families favoring the Union felt threatened and many left, making temporary homes in the Northern states, while others moved toward Texas and the southwest. Others remained, but they endured great hardships, not only from battles between those wearing the blue of the Union and the gray of the Confederacy, but from bushwhackers, who swore no allegiance except to that of violence.

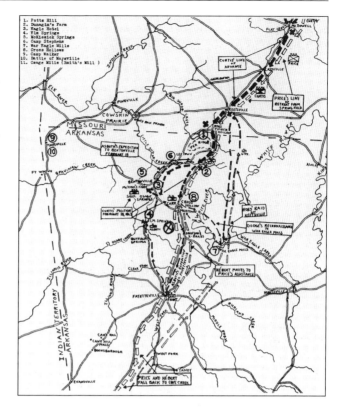

Troop Movements during Battle of Pea Ridge, February 1862. The black arrows are Union forces and white are Confederates. The encircled "X" is the location of Shiloh.

Americus V. Rieff organized a company of 91 men in the month of June 1861. It was known as Captain Rieff's Company in the Regiment of Arkansas Mounted Volunteers. Brigadier General Ben McCulloch called the volunteers into the service of the Confederate States of America for a term of three months from the date of enrollment. The company marched to Camp McRea Walker, a distance of 41 miles, arriving July 5, 1861.

John Holcombe, saw his son Jo volunteer for Arkansas State Militia Service, and also saw his son William and sons-in-law Francis Smiley, William Smiley, and John Stafford volunteer for Captain Reiff's Company. Joseph, the father of Springdale, served until Lee's surrender. When the war was over, he did not return immediately to Shiloh, but located with his wife in Hemstead County where he laid out the town of Mineral Springs and conducted business for four years.

After a Southern victory at Wilson Creek on August 10, the Arkansas 5th forces were discharged. The first regiment formed in Washington County was Brooks Cavalry, which afterwards became the Arkansas Confederate Cavalry, Company E, First Battalion, made up of men from in and around Shiloh under Captain William H. Brooks. This company was mustered into service on October 9, 1861, at Fayetteville.

By the fall of 1861, many Arkansas companies of fighting forces formed after Federal forces amassed their troops along the border of northwest Arkansas to

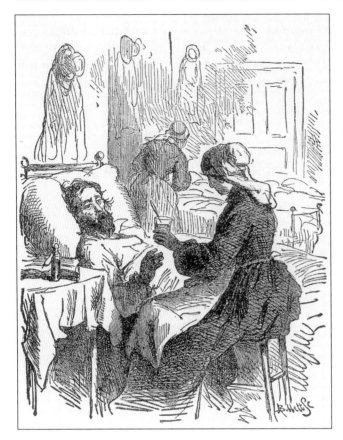

DRAWING OF CIVIL WAR HOSPITAL. *Often placed in large homes in the battle area, women volunteered to care for injured soldiers. This drawing is from an Arkansas school textbook dated 1935.*

concentrate their objective to protect Missouri. Their goal was to capture and control the area and relieve threats to the border states. The First Arkansas Cavalry Volunteers, a Federal (Union) company, was mustered into service on August 7, 1862, under Colonel LaRue Harrison. In the county, there were about 2,000 men in the Confederate Army and about 600 in the Federal Army.

Once again, John Holcombe's sons responded to the call of duty. Jo was engaged in securing supplies for the Quarter Master Corps; William Henry joined the 15th Arkansas Mounted Infantry of Northwest Company G; and John himself joined the 23rd Infantry Company H. Meanwhile, William Smiley joined the 15th Northwest Infantry Company G; Hiram Bynum joined the 34th Infantry Company A; Charles Wildes was inducted into 35th Arkansas Infantry Company F; Francis Smiley joined the 15th Northwest Infantry Company G; John Stafford enrolled in the 6th Arkansas Infantry Company I. The two youngest sons, Silas and George, were still minors living at home with their parents and older sister Dorothy.

Another pioneer of Shiloh, Evans Atwood, fought for the Confederacy and was captured by the Federals. He was not freed until the war was over, when he returned home to find that his wife had thought him dead and had remarried. Atwood sat down with her and her second husband and they decided she could take her choice of two of the Atwood children and leave with her husband. She did and was never heard from again. Atwood went away to study medicine and when he returned, he married again and reared a large family. The following is from a letter to Atwood from his sister Harriet Atwood Lichlyter, then living in Indiana, dated July 19, 1863:

> Dear Brother: I now seat myself to answer your most kind and beautiful letter which I received yesterday. I received three letters from Father's folks last May and one from Lucy Jane . . . Lucy and the children was well and hearty, and Father is broke up. The armies has took all of his stock from him and his wagon and he said he did not know what he would do, for that he has neither wagon nor money to bear his expenses. They told me that there was a great deal of sickness there [Shiloh] which took many to their graves. Mary Jane Lichlyter and William Loving and Steve Paggett was dead. And old Nelson Graham and Daniel Hinson was killed. So, I reckon I must tell you something about our moving. We was one month on the road, we had some bad luck. Albert Harrison is no more in this world, he died last April was a year on the road as we come here; and Father Lichlyter is no more. It is so sickly here, we expect to leave here day after tomorrow and go to Missouri where John and Crockett is and all our old neighbors. Evans, I have got one of the finest boys in Posey County, and we call it Simeon Jones. We have got us a good wagon and team. John and Crockett get the news from Arkansas all the time, and I think if we go there, that I can hear from Father's folks once in a while.

An entry in Evans Atwood's diary ended with the following:

> . . . A wife, children, father and mother, and sister and perhaps a brother at home in Arkansas not knowing that I am alive. Two years have almost passed since I saw them, and war is yet moving onward, recruiting for death, marching her thousands to the grave. How long will times thus go on? When shall the Angel of Death stay his arm of revenge and wing his flight to other realms, and Mercy, the Angel of Peace, shall revisit us with the olive branch entwined around her radiant brow, saying "Peace, be still." Then shall the weary soldier return to his friends and home of former days.

Atwood was a physician and an officer. He was a prisoner for four years at Sandusky, Ohio, and on Johnson's Island in the Chesapeake Bay. Being exchanged at Richmond, Virginia, at the war's close, barefooted and with no transportation, it took him four months to reach home a short distant southeast of Shiloh. In 1898, he moved to Texas.

D.D. Deaver related the following war story:

George William Deaver, a relative and John McCamey were on their way home on furlough from the Southern army. Some miles north of Elm Springs, they were overtaken by "damn Yankee" carpetbaggers, bushwhackers, or some other enemy, I know not who. Their horses were taken and the boys were killed. Their bodies, together with the saddles, were placed on a brush pile and burned. Soon as the news of their deaths reached Elm Springs, the sisters of each boy went after them in an ox cart. The bodies were wrapped in a sheet and buried in a single grave.

Sarah Elizabeth Banks, recalling the old days, told of living at Sycamore Springs during the Civil War. She saw General Price's army in retreat and witnessed her own father taken prisoner by the Federals while he was home on furlough. He was ill at the time of his capture. She recalled the following:

He had had hiccups for 15 days. We thought them caused by the cornbread diet that was almost the entire ration of the Confederate army in Northwest Arkansas. He was hurried off with some other Confederates who had been made prisoners, and we never expected to see or hear of him again. However, as he passed through Elm Springs he succeeded in leaving a message with Ab Wasson, who got it through to

MEN IN UNIFORM MARCHING DOWN EMMA AVENUE. *Some are carrying musical instruments. This picture was probably taken prior to World War I. (Courtesy of Bobbie Lynch and Shiloh Museum of Ozark History.)*

GRAND ARMY OF THE REPUBLIC, ON EMMA AVENUE, WITH OPERA HOUSE IN THE BACKGROUND, 1898. *The man with "X" below him is I. Tolbert Lane, mayor of Springdale from 1904 to 1907, 1908 to 1909, and 1914 to 1916. (Courtesy of Betty Lane Davis and Shiloh Museum of Ozark History.)*

our family. A second message came as he was on the march to a prison camp, this one being sent though Doc Arment.

The small pox hit the Banks household while her father was there and, though word was gotten to the doctor in Fayetteville, he must have been too busy, for he never came. Banks survived the dreaded pox and, as she was recovering, a squad of "Feds" appeared and headed for the smokehouse. She went to the window so they could see her scabs. Seeing how afraid they were, she opened the door and they took out.

Sarah Banks also remembered back to the days when keeping fires burning could be a real problem. If a fire went out and the coals grew cold, they had to be rekindled by igniting cotton by means of sparks from a flint. This was a hard chore for the women when the men weren't about. Having survived the hardships of early settlement, bushwhackers, the Civil War, and small pox, Banks lived a long life until one sunny autumn afternoon in 1949, when she bade farewell to this world.

The period immediately following the Civil War has been called disastrous for the state. The migration of carpetbaggers from the North and their cooperation with the scalawags of the South resulted in public corruption, wasted public funds, and fraud, according to *Government in Arkansas,* a book by the League of Women Voters. Following the years of Reconstruction after the Civil War, Arkansas drew up its constitution in 1874. The years of carpetbagger rule were gone and a new era awaited.

William Garland Ownbey as Captain at Fort Logan or Fort Roots, 1914. He served as a private in the Spanish-American War and, as a colonel, commanded the 142nd Field Artillery during World War I. (Courtesy of Marguerite Ownbey Walker and Shiloh Museum of Ozark History.)

Scars of the war did not heal quickly, however, as they were rubbed raw by a painful Reconstruction period. The sins of the carpetbaggers descended on all states that had seceded. It wasn't until August 15, 1905, that conditions were such that 160 Union veterans could gather in Springdale for a three-day reunion. It was time to move on and leave the war and its horrors behind. Balloon ascensions and parachute jumps were some of the featured entertainment. The *News* reported that Harry Phelan's parachute struck the smokestack of the canning factory and he broke his arm. For nearly 40 years, peace reigned. Shiloh became Springdale and prospered. The grumblings of war were not heard again until, on April 25, 1898, the United States declared war on Spain, following the sinking of the battleship *Maine* in Havana Harbor on February 15.

Two days later, Commodore George Dewey sailed from Hong Kong with Emilio Aguinaldo on board. Fighting began in the Phillipine Islands at the Battle of Manila Bay on May 1, where Commodore George Dewey reportedly exclaimed, "You may fire when ready, Gridley."

In May of 1898, Springdale celebrated Dewey's Manila victory. Company F left Springdale for Camp Dodge at Little Rock on May 11. There was a procession, a patriotic address by Dr. J.H. Amacher, the presentation of a flag, a response by Captain J.L. Long, and the march to the depot to take the midnight train. War actually began for the United States in Cuba in June when the Marines captured Guantanamo Bay and 17,000 troops landed at Siboney and Daiquiri, east of Santiago de Cuba, the second largest city on the island. The war ended with the signing of the Treaty of Paris on December 10, 1898. As a result, Spain lost its control over the remains of its overseas empire—Cuba, Puerto Rico, the Philippines, Guam, and other islands.

Company F never traveled beyond Georgia, remaining at Chicamauga Park until they were mustered out in late October 1898. Troops endured all the disadvantages of war except being under fire. Besides a measles epidemic, there was the constant threat of typhoid and malaria. Camp conditions were unsanitary and food was in short supply.

Representatives of Spain and the United States signed a peace treaty in Paris on December 10, 1898, established the independence of Cuba, ceded Puerto Rico and Guam to the United States, and allowed the victorious power to purchase the Philippines from Spain for $20 million. The war had cost the United States $250 million and 3,000 lives, of whom 90 percent had perished from infectious diseases.

One man who would play a huge part in the great war that lurked beyond the horizon was William Garland Ownbey, who was born in 1877, southeast of Springdale. He finished his education at the University of Arkansas and, for some years, was employed in the drug store of H.A. Daily, one of Springdale's pioneer druggists. He left Daily's to study pharmacy at the Ohio Institute of Pharmacy and opened his own drug store in town about 1898. He sold it only a short time before his death in 1928. Married in 1899 to Bertie Parker, he and his wife had two children, Julian Ownbey and Mrs. Lowrey Walker.

When the Spanish-American War broke out in 1898, Ownbey was a member of the National Guard and went to Chickamauga Park as a private in a company recruited in Springdale.

The unit of Company F disappeared when the state guard was reorganized in 1901 but was mustered by Captain Leon R. Smith of Fayetteville on January 16, 1914, to be known as Company A, 2nd Infantry. Later that year, as a result of the threat of war with Mexico, Ownbey received orders on May 1 to recruit the local company to fighting strength of 108 men. After brief camp training and reorganization into the First Arkansas Infantry, Company A of the 1st Battalion, 2nd Regiment, Arkansas National Guard, left for Fort Logan H. Roots on June 23, 1916.

In 1916, Ownbey recruited Company A of the Second Arkansas Infantry in Springdale and went with the company as a captain when it was sent to border service at Deming, New Mexico. After the company returned here, Ownbey was promoted to the rank of major. During training at Camp Beauregard he was promoted to the rank of lieutenant colonel.

In July 1916, Pancho Villa raided Columbus, New Mexico, and by August 8, Company A was sent to the Mexican border. Lieutenant Brogdon was put in charge of truck train Number 49 for six months. The men witnessed the triumphant return of General Black Jack Pershing's troops, and Lieutenant Brogdon hauled the signal corps out of Mexico when the America Expeditionary Forces were withdrawn. In March 1917, Company A returned from the Mexican border and Lieutenant Brogdon was discharged.

Emma Street became a regular parade ground as the entire town turned out regularly to bid the troops goodbye or welcome them home. Their comings and goings created all the reason the town needed to organize a parade. Yet the biggest of all battles was yet to come. For rumblings of a big war overseas disturbed the peaceful aftermath of victory down on the border.

In April 1917, the company was sent to Camp Pike where it was again reorganized as a part of the 142nd Field Artillery. Some declared that they were ready to go into battle against Kaiser Bill, and they almost got their wish. On August 5, 1917, the company was mobilized and began training in and around Springdale. The entire 142nd Field Artillery Regiment entrained at Beauregard and went to Camp Mills, Long Island, New York. Many had no uniforms and the only military items available for issue were blankets and mess kits. The battery trained with outdated Springfield rifles for no artillery equipment was available and none would be until after the battery was sent overseas.

In every home and business, sentiments ran high. Patriotism was at a premium. Flags waved from every post and door stoop as citizens placed their moral and

COMPANY A ON WAY TO MEXICAN BORDER, 1916. Company A is of the 1st Battalion, 2nd Regiment, Arkansas National Guard. (Courtesy of Mrs. L.W. Searcy and Shiloh Museum of Ozark History.)

CLARENCE E. BEELEY. He was the first soldier killed in World War I from Springdale. American Legion Post was named for him. (Courtesy American Legion and Shiloh Museum of Ozark History.)

emotional support firmly behind men who trained to do battle for their country. In April 1918, the city went over the top in the third Liberty loan drive, subscribing $108,000 toward the war effort.

Lieutenant Colonel W.G. Ownbey was ordered into active service and left for Fort Sill, Oklahoma. The draft registration took place June 5 at Camp Pike, and 204 local men between the ages of 21 and 31 were registered. Every mother and father, sister and wife, held their breath for what was surely to happen. In June the call came for volunteers from Battery A to go overseas as casualty replacements. Company A was formally mustered into the federal service on August 10. War had finally found the peaceful Ozark town, a war that would change it forever.

Troops sailed for France in the spring of 1918. Officers of the group were Lieutenant Colonel W.G. Ownbey, First Lieutenant B.B. Brogdon, First Sergeant W.P. Dixon, Second Lieutenant L.D. Petross ,and Quarter Master Sergeant Charles Kincaid. A youthful Clarence E. Beeley was among the troops, little aware of the tragic part he would play in the history of his hometown. The 142nd Field Artillery, of which Battery A of Springdale is a part, arrived in France on September 9, 1918. And back home the world stood still.

On March 1, Jno (John) P. King was the first man from Springdale to be wounded in service. The first Springdale man to die in World War I was Clarence

WORLD WAR I SOLDIERS IN FRONT OF SPRINGDALE HIGH SCHOOL, 1918. *As many as 204 local men between the ages of 21 and 31 registered for the draft and sailed for France that spring. (Courtesy Ruth Maggard and Shiloh Museum of Ozark History.)*

E. Beeley. He was born January 16, 1895, in Springdale and was killed in action in the Meuse-Argonne in France on October 3, just weeks before the signing of the Armistice on November 11.

Several women from Springdale served as nurses during World War I. One of those was Civil War soldier Evans Atwood's great-granddaughter, Eva Atwood, who had received nurses training in Little Rock. Eva was born on January 2, 1890, in Saline County, Arkansas. At the age of 18, she became a nurse and was the first and only nurse in the area in 1909 when she went to work for Dr. C.F. Perkins and Dr. Frank Young in Springdale. She spoke of how much typhoid fever there was in the Springdale area during the early 1900s, saying she nursed one family with five cases of typhoid at the same time. "I operated on a lot of kitchen tables and a lot of them didn't live," she told Becky Hall in an interview in 1975 for the *Springdale News*.

When World War I broke out, Eva's two brothers, Clyde and Charlie, went into the service, and she wanted to be with them. She was called to Camp Pike in 1917 to serve as a war nurse. While serving in France, she fell in love, but her fiancé was killed. Devastated by her loss, she never married and kept his picture on her dresser all her life. Eva was beloved by all who knew her. She once gave her shoes to a woman who came to her door barefooted. When asked why she gave away her own shoes, she replied, "Because there was snow on the ground and she had none. I have warm floors."

Eva later served as superintendent of nurses of Sparks Memorial Hospital in Fort Smith and of the State Tuberculosis Sanitarium. She was an administrator of Springdale Memorial Hospital and served as the first president of the Springdale Memorial Hospital. She was also the chairman for the First District of the American Legion, was active in the Veterans of Foreign Wars, and was a director for welfare of the Springdale Community Fund. She, Charles Elmer, and Ulyss Lovell began a tradition of putting flags on all the graves of World War I and World War II soldiers on Armistice Day and Memorial Day each year.

On June 26, 1919, Battery A returned to Springdale clad in overseas uniforms and wide smiles. The Fourth of July celebration that year was a joyous homecoming for all the boys who had returned safely. The American Legion Beeley Post was established in 1921 and named after Clarence E. Beeley. A home for the post was not built until 1934 when the American Legion Hut, Post 139, was constructed of native stone in 1934 and, on Sunday, August 26, dedicated to the young man who had given his life on foreign soil for the cause of freedom. No unit of the national guard existed again until 1955. In the 1930s, men joined units of the 142nd Field Artillery Regiment organized in Fayetteville and Rogers.

The 142nd Field Artillery Regiment was called to active duty for one year in January 1941 when the United States entered World War II and remained in federal service until late 1945. It lost its all-Arkansas personnel makeup during the war, as experienced artillery men, who were transferred to serve as cadets of newly formed units, were replaced by draftees, enlistees, and officers from other states.

In 1942, the post collected 825 pounds of precious scrap aluminum. Harold E. Henson reentered the Army as a major and, in 1943, the post collected 1,500 phonograph records for Springdale's Armed Forces. In 1944, the post put its weight behind the GI Bill of Rights for World War II veterans.

Following the war, a local veteran died suddenly, leaving a wife and 10 children. Members of the post pitched in, fed the wife and children, and built them a home. They were living in a converted chicken house with no plumbing or electricity.

WORLD WAR I SOLDIERS ON EMMA AVENUE. Colonel W.G. Ownbey is in center front. (Courtesy of Marguerite Ownbey Walker and Shiloh Museum of Ozark History.)

The family had only been residents three years and had asked for help from Eva Atwood, by then serving as adjutant of the local legion post. After the veteran's death, Atwood spearheaded the effort to take care of his family.

Part of the 142nd was reactivated in October 1946. In 1950, the men also saw duty in Korea and, later, served in Vietnam and the Gulf War. The Springdale National Guard Unit, Company B, 212th Signal Battalion, was organized in June 1955. A year later, the Springdale Armory was completed. The unit was included in the general reorganization of National Guard units in Arkansas and became Battery C, 3rd Howitzer Battalion, 142nd Field Artillery Group in June of 1959. On December 1, 1967, it was renamed Battery B, 1st Battalion, 142nd Field Artillery Group.

In 1963, the American Legion post became the Beeley-Johnson Post when a World War II soldier, Elmer Johnson Jr., who died of wounds in Brittany, France on September 12, 1944, was added to the post's name.

Eva Atwood continued to serve her community until March 28, 1974, when she passed on, leaving behind a legacy of love and compassion for her fellow man.

AMERICAN LEGION HUT, SPRINGDALE. *Built of native stone, the hut was dedicated and named for the first man to lose his life in World War I from Springdale on Sunday, August 26, 1934. (Courtesy of Washington County Historical Society and Shiloh Museum of Ozark History.)*

10. Ah, Prosperity

We're in one of the hottest spots in Arkansas, and we're going to get our fair share.
—Lee Zachary, Springdale Chamber of Commerce

On May 16, 1905, Italian Ambassador Baron des Planches appeared before throngs of cheering citizens in Springdale and urged the Italians, who had settled in nearby Tontitown, to cease their connections to the old world and Italy and embrace their United States homeland.

His speech set the trend, not only for those who had come from so far away, but also for those who had emigrated from the Carolinas, Tennessee, Kentucky, Georgia, and points east. All would put behind them their old ties and bind themselves to this rugged land in a way that would ensure the prosperity of their new home.

While the town grew tremendously in the first 100 years, that growth was nothing compared to what occurred when World War II ended and men returned home to create businesses, build homes, and start families.

The poultry industry exploded in importance. From 1941 to 1947, the total production of the entire state was near 15 million broilers annually, but, by 1950, that number had increased to nearly 50 million. Poultry processing and related food processing plants soon made the county one of the five most heavily industrialized counties in Arkansas. This was bound to cause problems, the largest of which was an inadequate supply of water. The advent of poultry processing plants and other local industry required more water. An adequate water supply soon became the first priority of city fathers. A drought that began in 1952 and continued through 1955 had reduced the flow at both springs, still the city's only water supply.

In 1954, the city laid 7.5 miles of pipeline to a new source of supply purchased on Osage Creek and Osage River, and a raw pumping station was built there. The lines provided a capacity of 2.3 million gallons per day that could be increased to 3.5 million gallons a day by the addition of another pump. It could be further impounded to produce 50 million gallons a day if demanded. Even this would not long be enough to supply the amazing growth in the region.

A very important authorization by Congress in 1954 allowed the construction of Beaver Lake under the Flood Control Act. Immediately, area leaders began to

BARON DE PLANCHES, 1905. *He is pictured here in the center of three men to the left of the group of children in Tontitown during the time he visited Springdale. (Courtesy of Shiloh Museum of Ozark History.)*

consider using the lake as a source of water. The census taken in 1960 showed the city's population had doubled in ten years, emphasizing the need for more water. Beaver Water District was originally a Springdale project, spearheaded by Joe M. Steele, founder of Steele Canning Company. Once Beaver Lake Dam was under construction, the city built its first industrial park as an incentive to prospective industries looking for a place to build. The Beaver Dam Water project would solve the water problems of the entire northwest Arkansas area for many years to come, as well as create a 31,000-acre lake, a boon to tourism in the future.

Construction of Beaver Lake reservoir and water treatment plant was completed in 1966. Beaver Water District is unique in that it operates on revenues from its own sales. The Corps of Engineers oversees the lake. Springdale built the first treatment facility for Beaver Lake water and started pumping from it in January 1966. Four cities, Springdale, Fayetteville, Rogers, and Bentonville, obtain their total water supply from the facility and the system also sells water to other systems in the two counties.

The town's first shopping center was begun in the summer of 1964. This step emphasized the gradual movement of trade away from downtown. In June of that year, the chamber of commerce Industrial Committee told 75 business and civic leaders that they were at the crossroads of industrial development. The subject of the statement was a committee proposal to establish a new precedent-setting industrial park in Springdale. The park would consist of an improved area of industrial sites to show industrial prospects. The $700,000 bond election to create such a park barely squeaked by the voters. The new industrial park fulfilled its promise, attracting scores of manufacturers to the city. Jones Truck Lines announced plans to build the most modern freight terminal in the nation on a 17-acre site between Emma and Huntsville Avenues. The trucking industry was to have an immediate and substantial impact on the city's economy.

At the same time, some 13 acres adjacent to the airport were broken up into four parcels and sold to aviation-oriented industries. A hatchery, a plant for the manufacture of aviation instruments, and a vending company made immediate use of three parcels of land.

Steele Cannery, founded by Joe Steele, grew to be one of the largest privately owned canning companies in the world, due in part to the introduction of Popeye Spinach in 1965. Joe's son Phillip had joined the company in 1957 and negotiated a contract with King Features Syndicate, owner of the Popeye cartoon character. Springdale quickly became the spinach capital of the world.

It wasn't until a major fire broke out in the First State Bank Building in April 1965 that renewed interest was sparked to expand the fire department. Seventeen volunteer firemen and five part-time officers were reclassified as firefighters by

Aerial View of 31,000-Acre Beaver Lake. This beautiful lake is the water supply for the northwest Arkansas area. (Courtesy of Shiloh Museum of Ozark History.)

the city council, and Mickey Jackson was hired as the city's first paid fire chief. A major fire at Tyson's Garage in November graphically illustrated the need for updated equipment.

In February 1966, a bond issue was approved and the fire department received $169,000 for expansion. The money bought a 1,000-gallons-per-minute snorkel and a pumper capable of delivering the same amount of water. It also funded two new substations, one on Sanders Avenue and the other on Dyer Street, paid for protective clothing for all firefighters, and bought a complete radio alerting system for volunteer and paid firemen. Following several increases in manpower, the fire department began operating the city ambulance service in 1967. After a severe fire in the main classroom building of Central Junior High in January 1971, a bond issue funded a $35,000 pumper truck for the fire department. By the end of 1972, it had five fire engines, a snorkel, and four ambulances. A rescue unit was inherited from the disbanded civil defense unit.

Meanwhile, the city had acquired matching funds to build a new library. The old one was closed and the enormous task of moving to the new building on the corner of Maple Avenue and South Pleasant Street began. A formal dedication of the Springdale Public Library was held in April of 1966.

On the night of June 11, 1970, a tornado ripped through Springdale with no warning other than a deafening roar. The vicious funnel tore a path of devastation

TORNADO DAMAGE IN ELMDALE AREA OF SPRINGDALE, JUNE 11, 1970. *It left one man dead, injured scores of others, and left a trail of destruction about a mile long and a quarter of a mile wide, causing millions of dollars in damage. (Courtesy of* Springdale News *and Shiloh Museum of Ozark History.)*

View from Johnson Avenue of Covered Spring Creek Channel through Downtown Area, 1974. The project began in 1973 and was completed in May 1975. (Courtesy of Shiloh Museum of Ozark History.)

across the northwest section of the city. It left one man dead, injured scores of others, and left a trail of destruction about 1 mile long and a quarter of a mile wide, causing millions of dollars in damage. The fire department transported the injured, conducted searches, and rescued victims. It also set up a search and rescue center. Springdale was declared a disaster area and United States Representative John Paul Hammerschmidt and United States Senator J. William Fulbright toured the area to inspect the damage.

The most spectacular fire in the city's history occurred in February 1976 when Central Grease and Protein on East Meadow Avenue burned. The fire, which was set by an arsonist, leveled the tall building, formerly a feed mill, and firemen were kept busy controlling the spread to adjoining industrial facilities. By 1978, the modernized department consisted of six radio dispatched engines, three ambulances manned by trained advanced EMTs, a reserve ambulance, a completely equipped rescue unit, a spare rescue vehicle, and an 18-foot rescue boat.

Four million tourists visited northwest Arkansas and Beaver Lake in 1977. The lake and its recreational facilities are credited as the main reason tourism is the second largest economic boon to the area. Floods continued to be a major problem because of Spring Creek cutting through the center of town. In October of 1965, an urban renewal project began in the city. The first step was to rehabilitate or demolish substandard business structures in the downtown area

Drainage of Spring Creek, Part of the Urban Renewal Project, 1973. By 1974, the area of Springdale and Fayetteville had moved into the top 200 urban areas in the United States. (Courtesy of Shiloh Museum of Ozark History.)

and homes in a widespread area. The Corps of Engineers agreed to work with urban renewal to widen and deepen the Spring Creek channel from Old Missouri Road downtown and beyond to Shiloh Street. The project was funded by both agencies and the city at a cost of more than $2 million.

Billed as one of the fastest growing cities in the country during the last half of the 1960s, official population figures released in January 1971 by the United States Bureau of Census proved the claim. A special census in 1974 revealed that Springdale's population had grown to 19,962, and the Fayetteville-Springdale metropolitan area moved into the nation's top 200 urban areas due to a population growth rate four times the national average. During the period between 1966 and 1974, the city had increased from 11 to 18 square miles and the assessment on real estate property had grown from $12 million to $30 million.

A study done in 1974 to determine the effects of trucking found, using 12 companies for evaluation, that 1,220 persons in town were employed in trucking. The total gross revenue for seven Springdale trucking firms was $88.83 million. In 1980, the Sun Company purchased Jones Truck Lines and a new president, John Karlberg, took over, only the third president in the company's long history. Following several years of expansion after its sale to the Sun Company, the Jones Truck Lines closed its doors in July of 1991 and filed for bankruptcy. Janet Hawkins wrote in the *Morning News* that "deregulation and questionable financial maneuvering by upper level management team which had bought the company, led to its liquidation."

Though Highway 71 was paved in four lanes from Springdale to Fayetteville in 1961, a north-south four-lane highway from the Missouri border to Interstate 40 at Alma, which had been under consideration since the early 1970s, continued to be only so much talk. Interstate 540, which connects northwest Arkansas to Interstate 40 near Fort Smith, opened in January 1999. The Arkansas Highway Department says the daily vehicle count on I-540 is 16,000 per day. Both the highway and a new airport provide easier access to the region.

While plants continued to announce expansion programs, 1974 became a record year for construction in Springdale. As many as 308 building permits, at a value of $11,969,492, were issued. Among them was Springdale Memorial Hospital's $5 million expansion in June. Under the guidance of Lee Zachary, the chamber of commerce helped bring an incredible growth of industry into the area. By the early 1990s, however, both Lee Zachary and Mayor Charles McKinney agreed that the city no longer had the work force to readily accommodate any large expansions. Future economic development hinged on expanding the work force and, to do that, affordable housing had to be made available.

Charles McKinney was elected mayor of Springdale in 1978 and would serve the city for two decades in that office, the longest term one man had ever served

CHARLES McKINNEY, MAYOR OF SPRINGDALE FROM 1978 THROUGH 1998. *Upon McKinney's death in 2002, it was said that the city of Springdale had McKinney to thank for the prosperity they enjoy today. (Courtesy of Shiloh Museum of Ozark History.)*

as mayor. He is said to have done more to establish jobs in the area than any other mayor in its history.

The Frisco Railroad merged with Burlington Northern in 1980. The importance of the railroad to the city's progress resulted in Burlington Northern Railroad consolidating its northwest Arkansas freight operations in December 1982. The old depot was torn down that year and a plain metal building was put into use. The last passenger train ran in September of 1965, but approximately 8,000 railroad freight cars were being off-loaded by 1982, more than were handled in all other communities in both Benton and Washington Counties. In 1986, the Arkansas & Missouri Railroad bought Burlington Northern and, since 1990, has included passenger excursion service with its freight runs between Springdale and Van Buren.

The Wal-Mart phenomenon cannot be ignored in a story of boom times in this area. Sam Walton opened a Walton Five and Dime in nearby Bentonville in 1950 and, by the end of the 1960s, there were 18 Wal-Marts across Arkansas. By 1985, 753 Wal-Mart stores covered 20 states in the South. Its growth continues to be extraordinary.

HARVEY AND BERNICE JONES. Harvey, pioneer trucker, founded Jones Truck Lines and his wife, Bernice, established the Jones Center for Families. (Courtesy of Shiloh Museum of Ozark History.)

JONES CENTER FOR FAMILIES. *This facility houses an Olympic-sized pool, several sports arenas and meeting rooms, and is free to the public. (Courtesy of Jones Center for Families.)*

Harp's grocery stores expanded over the years until, by 1991, the chain had 22 stores in Arkansas and Oklahoma. Harp's IGA was Springdale's first supermarket. In August 2001, Harps, owned primarily by the Harp family for 71 years, became employee owned.

Northwest Arkansas Regional Airport (XNA) opened on November 1, 1998, at Highfill, after eight years in the planning stage. Earlier ventures to create such an airport in 1954 and the early 1970s had floundered. The success of this final attempt to build an airport miles away from a city of any size came about largely through the efforts of the Walton and Tyson families. Residents throughout the area resisted its construction and, in particular, resented the resultant closure of Fayetteville's City Airport at Drake Field. Today, the airport's runways sprawl through pastures in the remote rural countryside, with efforts underway to commercialize the area to make it more attractive to business travelers.

Harvey Jones and his wife, Bernice, had founded the Jones Foundation in 1957 to provide scholarship money to Springdale High School students. The foundation also donated gifts to the University of Arkansas and donated land worth more than $220,000 to the school district.

Following her husband's death, Bernice built the Bernice and Harvey Jones Center for Families in Springdale and, in an unprecedented move, threw open the doors of the huge sports and meeting-room complex to everyone who wanted to use it. The center is recognized as the most complete family center in the entire state, offering recreation and education for everyone from toddlers to seniors. The

220,000-square-foot center was funded entirely by Bernice Jones. Etched on the front door are the words, "All are welcome who behave as ladies and gentlemen."

In a move to attract larger retailers, the four largest cities of northwest Arkansas merged their populations into a Metropolitan Statistical Area (MSA) in 1993. The population of two adjacent counties that had no shopping malls were merged with Washington and Benton Counties to come up with a retail trade area figure that more accurately represented the number of people who shopped in the two-county MSA. The result was 113,409 people in the two-county MSA and 241,180 in the four-county retail trade area. That figure brought the area to the magic number that national retailers look at before committing to growth in an area. To continue to provide quality services to the increased population, the city passed a 1 percent sales tax increase in the 1990s to provide capital improvement funds. A $4.4-million project began in 1994 to expand city hall, the police department, and the fire department.

Mayor Jerre Van Hoose considers the city's biggest problem today to be the lack of retail businesses that would generate more sales tax. A shortage in sales tax revenue has led to a tighter city budget, which means firemen went without raises in 2001. Van Hoose also cites a lack of a major east-west road as adding to the snarl of traffic that plagues drivers.

Though population growth of the 1990s has drastically changed the city's ethnic makeup, it didn't seem to impact the overall crime rate, which has steadily decreased. In 1990, the Hispanic population was 446 people, or 1.5 percent of the city's total population of 29,941. By 2001, Benton and Washington Counties had the highest number of Hispanics in the state, with 12,932 living in Washington County. Of that total, Springdale registered 8,948 Hispanic residents, almost one-fourth of the city's total population. Because of the high influx of Hispanic and other immigrant students, Springdale budgeted $1.1 million for English as a Second Language (ESL) teacher salaries and programs for the 2001–2002 school year.

Over the past five years, the city has committed itself to new parks and high-quality recreation facilities. The J.B. Hunt Trucking firm offered the city a good deal on land for the new park. Springdale spent $2.5 million to renovate a Youth Center; about $2 million in upgrades to Murphy Park; around $3 million developing J.B. Hunt Park, a new 110-acre complex on the city's north end; and $4.1 million on a new aquatic park. The late 1980s saw the 75-acre Randal Tyson Recreational Complex built.

In 1995, Springdale Memorial Hospital completed a $32.2 million expansion project that included the Harvey Jones Patient Tower, the Jones Clinic professional office building, and a three-story parking garage, at the same time becoming the Northwest Medical Center. It merged with Bates Medical Center in Bentonville to form Northwest Health System in 1996 and changed from a non-profit facility to a privately owned facility, making many new programs and advanced medical treatments available. The hospital had undergone many changes prior to that. Cardiac care was first offered in 1979 when cardiologist Charles Inlow joined the staff. An Air Evac system was installed in 1991. In 1993,

Inlow performed the first arterial stent surgery and excimer laser angioplasty. A neo-natal unit was added that same year. In 1996, the medical center became affiliated with Northwest Family Care, a primary care clinic. Since then, eight more facilities of this type have been opened.

Northwest Arkansas Radiation Therapy Institute (NARTI) is a non-profit cancer treatment center. Its formation was first discussed in 1983 and a steering committee began a study to provide more information. Nine hospitals in the area provided seed money for NARTI and the Jones Foundation contributed $1 million to the project. By 1995, over 5,000 patients had been treated. No one seeking treatment is ever turned away for lack of funds.

In a city with no planning department until 1996, Springdale has faced a case of playing catch-up and overcoming the lack of planning of the past few decades. Often, zoning areas overlap, which causes residences and businesses to collide. In 2002, members of the city council promised to approve a new and better land use plan. A year-long expansion program completed in 2000 brought the public library up to the standards demanded by today's patrons. Known as "The Library in the Park," its 43,000-square-foot building offers a relaxing atmosphere. In an effort to keep up with the spiritual needs of parishioners, churches in Springdale have acquired more than $8 million in building permits since 1998. It is easy to imagine the pleasure John Holcombe would experience if he could behold the many beautiful places of worship in Springdale today. Living up to its name, his beloved Shiloh has truly become a city of churches.

SPRING VALLEY BAPTIST CHURCH, 1981. *This is an example of many of the rural churches that served the surrounding communities and continue to do so. (Courtesy of Shiloh Museum of Ozark History.)*

The last decade also brought about a huge rise in business flying in and out of Springdale's small airport. With 130 aircraft based there, including eight jets and three helicopters, the airport offers air freight, an air ambulance, charter flights, flight instruction, and aircraft rental. J.B. Hunt Transport, the Lowell-based trucking firm, maintains a large hangar for its jet aircraft.

The Springdale School District booted up technology during the 1990s, adding 2,000 computers throughout the district. Shiloh Christian School is the only private Christian school in Springdale that offers classes through the 12th grade. Lee and Walker elementary were named national Blue Ribbon Schools in May 1997, joining others in the district who have been so honored: Smith, Parson's Hill, and Westwood.

Three new schools were built in the 1990s, and, in the year 2000–2001, 700 new pupils enrolled in the schools. Over the next ten years, a $102 million building plan calls for the construction of four elementary schools, a junior high, a middle school, and a second high school. Generous donations to help the overburdened schools have come from mega-companies, such as Harp's, George's, Tyson's (with a donation in cash of $8 million), and Harvey and Bernice Jones, whose charitable trust has given $100 million to schools, hospitals, and family charities statewide in the past ten years. The problem is where will the land be found for these schools of the future?

With a population that nearly doubled in the decade between 1990, when it was 29,941, to 2000, when it reached 45,798, the city issued residential building permits for $69 million in 2000 and $63 million in 2001. A desire to live the quiet rural life has attracted tens of thousands of residents to the area. Families move here from Chicago and Detroit, from the crowded metropolitan areas of the east and west coast and foreign locales, all searching for a simpler, less hectic existence. Ironically, their arrival in such great numbers threatens the very way of life that attracted them to Springdale in the first place. Perhaps a balance can be reached, but it appears that the northwest corner of Arkansas is fast-becoming a metro-plex to rival any that these residents may have left behind.

The *Springdale News* serves the area today as the daily *Springdale Morning News,* now owned by the Donrey Media Group and published daily. Edward Stafford, son of its founder John P. Stafford, passed away in 1957.

Former longtime mayor Charles McKinney passed away in March 2002. He was lauded as a living legacy. He never lost his popularity as the city's leader, according to an editorial in *The Northwest Arkansas Times* following his death. The editorial concluded, "The people there [Springdale] know they have McKinney to thank for the Springdale they now enjoy, and the continued success of that city stands as a living legacy to his memory."

There appears to be no end to the accomplishments of those who live, love, work, and play in this place once known as Shiloh, founded by a handful of courageous pioneers with a magnificent dream.

Bibliography

Books

Gerstaker, Freiderick. *In the Arkansas Backwoods*. English translation by James William Miller. Originally published in Germany, 1854.

Goodspeed's History of Arkansas. Chicago: Goodspeed Publications, 1886–1887.

Holcomb, Herbert Gordon. *John Holcombe's Odyssey: A Story of a Nineteenth Century American Pioneer*. Springdale, 1999.

Schoolcraft, Henry R. *Journal of a Tour into the Interior of Missouri and Arkansaw*. Performed in the Years 1818 and 1819. London: Richard Phillips and Company, 1821.

School Days, School Days: The History of Education in Washington County, 1830–1950. Compiled by members of the Washington County Rural Teachers Association. Printed at Fayetteville High School West Campus Area Vocational-Technical School.

Shiloh Museum of Ozark History. *Washington County History*. 1989.

Strausberg, Stephen F. *From Hills and Hollers: Rise of the Poultry Industry in Arkansas*. Fayetteville: Arkansas Agricultural Experiment Station, University of Arkansas, 1995.

Vaughan, Bruce. *Emma We Love You*. Springdale: Shiloh Museum of Ozark History, 1994.

Newspapers

Springdale News
  Golden Anniversary Edition, 1937

Bibliography

75th Anniversary Edition, 1962
Centennial Edition, 1978
Progress Edition, 1982
Progress Edition, 1985
Progress Edition, 1991
Progress Edition, 1997
Progress Edition, 2001

Arkansas Democrat Gazette
Winds of Change Edition, 2002

Periodicals

Washington County Historical Society Quarterly

Flashback issues: April 1955; November 1968; May 1970; February 1974; November 1974; August 1976; February 1977; May 1978; February 1985; and August 1999.

Shiloh/Springdale Centennial Celebration, 1878–1919.

LICHLYTER'S STORE INTERIOR, 1950. *From left to right are Grace Baggett, Joy Payne, and Leo Lichlyter. (Courtesy of Joy Payne and Shiloh Museum of Ozark History.)*

INDEX

Arcade Hotel, 45, 56–58, 92
Arkansas & Missouri Railroad, 43, 152
Atwood, Eva, 89, 142, 144
Atwood, Evans, 131, 134, 135, 142
Bank of Springdale, 59, 60, 71, 83, 114
Beeley, Clarence E., 126, 141–144
Berry, Judge Millard, 35, 36, 53, 59, 62, 77, 82–85, 97, 112, 119
Brogdon & Company, 65
Brogdon, W.B., 36, 65, 91, 94
Brown, Jeff D., 103–106, 108
Bryan, William Jennings, 123, 125
Burlington Northern, 152
Butterfield Stage Line, 16, 17, 41, 42, 55
churches
   Central Presbyterian Church, 77, 118
   Elm Springs Methodist Church, 31
   First Baptist Church, 6, 25, 30, 38, 39
   First Methodist Church, 25, 29
   Liberty Baptist Church, 25
   First Presbyterian Church, 25, 26
   Shiloh Primitive Baptist Church, 17, 20, 22, 24, 25, 43, 52
Claypool, Will, 91
Commercial Hotel, 58
Deaver, Emma Dupree, 61
Deaver, James P., 59–61, 84, 115
Fitzgerald, James, 15
Fitzgerald, John, 15, 16
Fitzgerald Station, 42, 74, 75
Fremont, General John C., 44
Frisco House, 58, 62

Frisco (San Francisco/St. Louis) Railroad, 42–45, 52, 58, 92, 97, 99, 100, 152
George, C.L., 106, 107
Gladden Hotel, 16, 42, 55, 56–58, 78, 88
Harris, J.R., 59, 67, 82
Haxton Woolen Mill, 66, 67, 69, 70, 88
Holcombe, John, 17, 19–24, 26, 42, 52, 54, 59, 133, 134, 155
Holcomb, Joseph, 18, 21, 22, 27, 34, 52, 58, 61, 62, 66, 78, 118, 133, 134
Howard, Guy, 128, 129
Hunt, J.B., 50, 154, 156
Hyden, Wayne, 116, 117
Jones, Bernice, 127, 152, 153, 154
Jones, Harvey, 48, 49, 152, 153, 154
Jones Truck Lines (JTL), 48, 49, 147, 150, 152
Lichlyter, Dick, 67, 87
Lovelady Stage Stop and Inn, 16, 42, 53, 55, 57
Ludwig, O.C., 61, 118
Lynch's Prairie Station, 16, 42, 74
McKinney, Charles, 120, 128, 129, 151, 156
Nation, Carrie, 124, 125
Ownbey, Carl A., 65
Ownbey, Colonel W.G., 46, 65, 77, 115, 119, 138, 139, 141, 143
Parsons, Thurman "Shorty," 126
Petross, Chism, 2, 52, 59, 67, 80
Phillips, S.R. "Cy," 116
Putman, Bennett, 25, 55, 76
Robinson, Joe, 46, 50, 128, 129

159

Index

Shinn, Josiah H., 35, 36, 123, 124
Sisco, Dr. C.P., 88
Smith, Dr. A.C., 46, 71, 125
Smyer, C.L., 79, 80
Springdale News, 31, 39, 42, 47, 50, 54, 55, 58, 62–64, 68, 71, 72, 74, 77, 78, 80, 82, 84, 86, 88, 91, 93–96, 113, 114, 118, 121, 122, 125, 138, 142, 148, 156
Springdale Roller Mill, 67, 80, 82
Stafford, John Pleasant, 24, 61–64, 77, 92, 124, 125, 133, 134, 156

Steele Canning Company, 98, 146, 147
Steele, Joe M., 98, 108, 146, 147
Todhunter, Shelby, 113
Tyson, Don, 108, 109, 111
Tyson, John, 51, 108, 109, 111
Van Hoose, Peter P., 32
Van Winkle, Peter, 44
Young, Dr. John, 53

A Crowd on Emma Avenue in the 1930s. By then, the street was paved, there were electric street lights, and the town was growing rapidly. This gathering could have been an auction or sale of some kind. (Courtesy of Wayne Barrack and Shiloh Museum of Ozark History.)